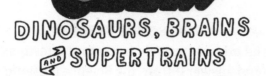

SUPER GEEK!

DINOSAURS, BRAINS & SUPERTRAINS

Glenn Murphy is the author of around twenty popular science books aimed at kids and teenagers. He received his masters in science communication from London's Imperial College of Science, Technology and Medicine. He wrote his first book, *Why Is Snot Green?*, while working at the Science Museum, London. In 2007 he moved to the United States. He now lives and works in sunny, leafy North Carolina, with his wife Heather, his son Sean and two unfeasibly large cats.

Al Murphy has drawn pictures for lots of people, including the *Guardian*, the *New York* magazine and the BBC, but his favourite thing to do is to draw for fun while listening to music and eating chocolate. He likes tomato soup with melted cheese and takes his tea with milk and one sugar.

He grew up in Old York (England) and now lives in New York (America) with his girlfriend Annie.

SUPER GEEK!

DINOSAURS, BRAINS AND SUPERTRAINS

GRARRR!

THIS. IS. A.M.A.Z.I.N.G.

IS HE HUNTING US LIKE A CHEETAH OR A HYENA?

WHO CARES?

SUPER GEEK!

FIZZ

BUBBLE

BY THE AUTHOR OF 'WHY IS SNOT GREEN?'

GLENN MURPHY

ILLUSTRATED BY AL MURPHY

MACMILLAN CHILDREN'S BOOKS

First published 2013 by Macmillan Children's Books
a division of Macmillan Publishers Limited
20 New Wharf Road, London N1 9RR
Basingstoke and Oxford
Associated companies throughout the world
www.panmacmillan.com

ISBN 978-1-4472-2716-8

1 3 5 7 9 8 6 4 2

A CIP catalogue record for this book is available from
the British Library.

Printed and bound by CPI Group (UK) Ltd, Croydon CR0 4YY

PICTURE CREDITS

t = top; b = bottom, r = right, l = left

25bl Glenn Murphy. All other images Shutterstock.com. Photographers: pages 9tl Esteban
De Armas; 9tr Andrew Meyer; 9bl Kostyantyn Ivanyshen; 9br Ozja; 12tl Andrew Meyer;
12tr Leonello Calvetti; 12bl DM7; 12br Linda Bucklin; 25br Linda Bucklin; 25tr outdoorsman;
25br Aron Armas; 28tl Ivan Kuzman; 28tr Willyam Bradberry; 28bl Jacek Chabraszewski;
28br Vittorio Bruno; 41tl cristapper; 41tr Ollirg; 41bl wdeon; 41br Arnan208; 44tl Koi88;
44tr Ignacio Salavenia; 44bl Harry Hu; 44br Graeme Shannon; 50t Max Earey; 50b Galina
Barskaya; 51t Ervin Monn; 51b Fedor Selivanov; 57tl jennyt; 57tr Martha Dean; 57bl l4lcol2;
57br James Steidl; 60tl stocker1970; 60tr Yusuke Sugahara, Tokyo University, Japan;
60bl Lee Prince; 60br Raif Siemieniec.

To Sean – welcome to the world, matey.
Trust me – it's gonna be fun.

Thanks to:

Deborah Bloxham and Gaby Morgan – for their encouragement and editing skills

Al Murphy for the superb artwork. I guess all Murphys ARE awesome

Lisa and Kristin Allred-Draper. Lisa – you are a wonderful friend; Kristin – I fully expect you to score 100% on this book

Mum, Dad, Lorn, Kev, Heath, Julie and the girls – thinking of you, always

Russ Campbell and the Burroughs Wellcome Fund – for keeping me in work between books

The NC Systema crew – for keeping me sane between books

Henry Walker and the students of the Carolina Friends School – always an inspiration.

CONTENTS

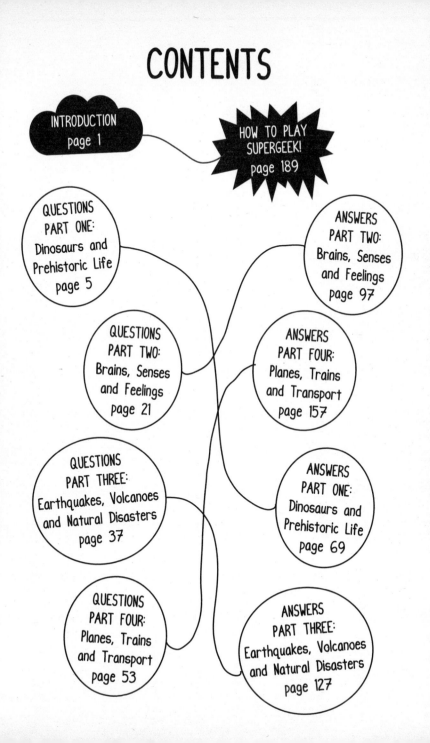

Introduction

It is the twenty-first century, and ours is a world ruled by **science** and **technology**.

Gone are the days when we hid our nerdy knowledge of computers.

No more must we cower behind our desks when we talk of androids and space travel.

It's a lightning-fast world, where new animal species are found every week, new technologies invented every minute and new web updates sent every second.

Without us, humanity has no hope of keeping up. The world *needs* us nerds. It cannot survive without the wisdom of the quick-witted geek.

But how much do *YOU* really know about the science that matters?

Could **you** tell an *apatosaurus* from an *ankylosaurus*?
Do **you** know the difference between *tsunami* and a *tornado*?
Could **you** tell us where your *blind spot* is, how many *passengers* fit on an *A380* or how many *taste buds* are on the average human tongue?

Challenge yourself. Challenge your friends. Only the true boffs will pass the test. Only the wise will succeed.

Only one shall be crowned . . .

SuperGeek!

How to use this book

SuperGeek is both a book *and* a game.

As a book, you can read it, cover to cover. Or you can dip in and out, starting with the chapter or theme you're most interested in. After reading a question, choose an answer, then turn to the Answers section in the second half of the book to check your choice and learn more.

There are more than 160 questions in this book, arranged into four themed chapters, with puzzles and fun stuff in between. Along the way, you'll learn all sorts of fascinating things about:

• dinosaurs and prehistoric life
• human brains and senses
• earthquakes, volcanoes and natural disasters
• cars, trains, planes and the future of transport.

Before long, you'll be stunning your friends and relatives with your new-found knowledge. Read the whole set of *SuperGeek* books, and become a mighty brainbox to be reckoned with!

But you can also *play* this book like a game – trying to get the highest quiz score possible, and perhaps earn yourself the coveted *SuperGeek* title.

So who should you play it with, and how do you play?

As for the *who* – that's entirely up to you.

- You can play with friends, either head-to-head, or in teams.
- You can play with your family, calling out the question from the back seat of the car during a road trip.
- You can play with your classmates, pitting one half of the class against the other.
- You can even play alone – pitting your wits against the clock, rather than an opponent.

How you play the game depends on the number of players, and whether you're playing in teams, or individually. To find out more about how to play *SuperGeek* – including how to score and rank your players – turn to page 189 at the back of the book.

In any case, I hope you enjoy this book. A whole world of geek-tastic knowledge awaits you. So whether you're reading, playing or battling, it's time to turn the page and **get stuck in** . . .

QUESTIONS

PART ONE: DINOSAURS AND PREHISTORIC LIFE

Do you know your *ankylosaurs* from your *allosaurs*? Which way the scales would tip if you weighed an *apatosaur* and a *blue whale*? What a *megalodon* is, and why you wouldn't want to meet one at the beach?

Let's get pre-historic!

Answers start on page 69.

SUPERGEEK: QUESTIONS

>>>>>>>>>>>>>>>>>>>>>>>>>>>>>>>

A: MEGA-BRAIN QUESTIONS

1. Which plant-eating dinosaur had a set of thick triangular plates running down its back?

a) Stegosaurus
b) Triceratops
c) Allosaurus
d) Iguanadon

2. How many horns did an adult *Triceratops* have?

a) one
b) two
c) three
d) five

3. What did male *Dimetrodons* (sailback lizards) use their sails for?

a) to sail across lakes and rivers
b) to warm up quicker in the sunshine
c) to attract female Dimetrodons
d) both (b) and (c)

>>>>>>>>>>>>>>>>>>>>>>>>>>>>>>>

4. What kind of animal was a *Megalodon*?

a) a huge meat-eating dinosaur
b) a huge prehistoric shark
c) a huge woolly mammoth
d) a sabre-toothed tiger

5. What does the name 'Dinosaur' really mean?

a) king lizard
b) deadly lizard
c) awesome lizard
d) dead lizard

6. Which of the following could dinosaurs NOT do?

a) run
b) jump
c) swim
d) fly

7. Most dinosaur species ate:

a) plants
b) meat
c) people
d) other dinosaurs

8. What was the largest, most ferocious carnivorous (meat-eating) dinosaur called?

a) Allosaurus
b) Tyrannosaurus
c) Gigantosaurus
d) Spinosaurus

9. The dinosaur with the longest name is called *Micropachycephalosaurus*. What does that mean?

a) tiny lizard
b) thick-headed lizard
c) tiny thick-headed lizard
d) big thick-headed lizard

10. Which family of flying reptiles soared above the dinosaurs for over 100 million years?

a) Aerosaurs
b) Pterosaurs
c) Glidasaurs
d) Plesiosaurs

B: PICTURE PUZZLE 1

What is it?

Name the animal in each of these pictures:

C: QUICK-FIRE QUESTIONS

	1	2	3	5
11. How many horns did a *Pentaceratops* have?	☐	☐	☐	☐
12. How wide, in centimetres, was the smallest known dinosaur egg?	☐	☐	☐	☐
13. How tall, in metres, was a fully grown *Velociraptor*?	☐	☐	☐	☐
14. How many feet did all *Therapod* dinosaurs walk on?	☐	☐	☐	☐
15. How wide, in metres, was the average *Pterodactyl*'s wingspan?	☐	☐	☐	☐

	13	17	30	100
16. How heavy, in tonnes, was an adult *Brachiosaurus*?	☐	☐	☐	☐
17. How many African elephants would weigh as much as an adult *Brachiosaurus*?	☐	☐	☐	☐
18. How tall, in metres, was an adult *Brachiosaurus*?	☐	☐	☐	☐
19. How many years could a Sauropod live before dying of old age?	☐	☐	☐	☐
20. Roughly how many bones were there in the neck of a *Diplodocus*?	☐	☐	☐	☐

	30	50	100	1,000
21. How heavy, in tonnes, was *Seismosaurus*?	☐	☐	☐	☐
22. How heavy, in tonnes, was *Apatosaurus*, largest of the *Pterosaurs*?	☐	☐	☐	☐
23. How many years did the average *Tyrannosaurus* live?	☐	☐	☐	☐
24. How fast, in miles per hour, could an *Ornithomimid* (ostrich-mimic) run?	☐	☐	☐	☐
25. Roughly how many known species of dinosaur are there?	☐	☐	☐	☐

	None	Half	Most	All
26. Of all known dinosaur fossils, how many were discovered by amateurs?	☐	☐	☐	☐
27. Of all dinosaur species, how many were found within the last 20 years?	☐	☐	☐	☐
28. Of all known dinosaur species, how many walked on two legs?	☐	☐	☐	☐
29. In how many of America's 50 states have dinosaurs been found?	☐	☐	☐	☐
30. How many dinosaur species still survive today?	☐	☐	☐	☐

D: PICTURE PUZZLE 2

Odd one out

Which one doesn't belong here, and why?

E: MORE MEGA-BRAIN QUESTIONS

31. During which time period did the dinosaurs first emerge?

a) Permian (from 300 million to 250 million years ago)
b) Triassic (from 250 million to 200 million years ago)
c) Jurassic (from 200 million to 145 million years ago)
d) Cretaceous (from 145 million to 65 million years ago)

32. During which time period did most of the dinosaurs die out?

a) Permian (from 300 million to 250 million years ago)
b) Triassic (from 250 million to 200 million years ago)
c) Jurassic (from 200 million to 145 million years ago)
d) Cretaceous (from 145 million to 65 million years ago)

33. Which family of animals lived alongside the dinosaurs in the Jurassic age?

a) turtles
b) crocodiles
c) insects
d) all of the above

34. A person who studies dinosaurs is known as:

a) a dinosaurologist
b) a palaeobotanist
c) a palaeontologist
d) a herpetologist

35. How large was the average dinosaur?

a) the size of a mouse
b) the size of a car
c) the size of a bus
d) the size of a house

36. In which place have the most species of dinosaur been discovered?

a) UK
b) North America
c) China
d) Australia

37. On how many of the world's seven continents have dinosaur fossils been found?

a) three
b) five
c) six
d) seven

38. What size, roughly, was the brain of an adult Stegosaurus?

a) the size of a peanut
b) the size of a walnut
c) the size of an orange
d) the size of a basketball

39. Which of the following were definitely NOT part of a Tyrannosaur's diet?

a) Hadrosaurs
b) Triceratops
c) Dimetrodons
d) other Tyrannosaurs

40. Which dinosaur family includes the tallest known dinosaur species?

a) therapods
b) sauropods
c) ornithopods
d) lankypods

PREHISTORIC PUZZLER

Use the clues to complete this tricky, dino-friendly crossword puzzle.

Across

2) Five-horned cousin of Triceratops (13)
3) Giant prehistoric shark (9)
4) Flying reptile of the Cretaceous age (9)
6) This sail-backed carnivore was larger and meaner than *T. Rex* (11)
8) Aquatic reptile of the Jurassic age; looks like the Loch Ness Monster (10)
9) Famous sail-backed Therapsid of the Permian age (10)
10) The study of dinosaurs (13)

Down

1) Time period AFTER the Jurassic (10)
5) Time period BEFORE the Jurassic (8)
7) 'Earthquake lizard'; largest of the Sauropods (12)

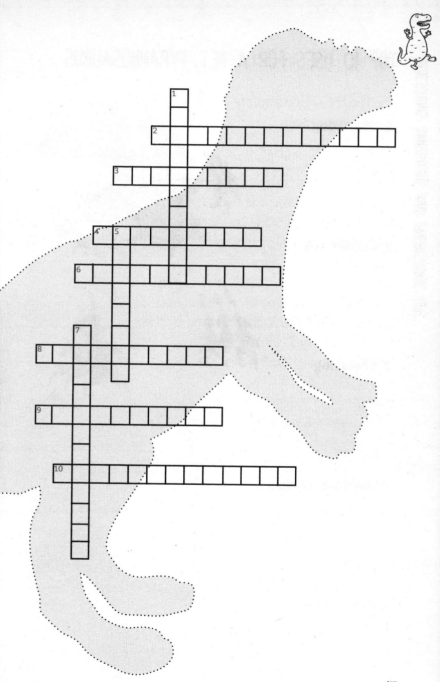

TOP 10 USES FOR A PET TYRANNOSAURUS

1. Guard dog

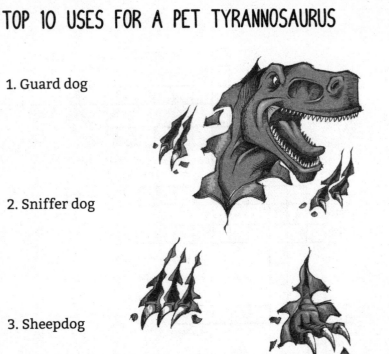

2. Sniffer dog

3. Sheepdog

4. Paper shredder

5. Car crusher

6. Team mascot

7. School bus

8. Teacher repellent

9. Kitchen waste disposal

10. Traffic warden disposal

QUESTIONS

PART TWO: BRAINS, SENSES AND FEELINGS

Do you know where your *cochlea* is? How many *cells* are in your brain? What your *sixth*, *seventh* and *eighth* senses are?

Time to *really* test that brain . . .

Answers start on page 97.

SUPERGEEK: QUESTIONS

>>>>>>>>>>>>>>>>>>>>>>>>>>>>>>>>

A: MEGA-BRAIN QUESTIONS

1. Which colours do most colourblind people have trouble telling apart?

a) reds and blues
b) reds and greens
c) blues and yellows
d) all of them

2. What are the five basic tastes our tongues can detect?

a) sweet, sour, bitter, fruity and spicy
b) sweet, sour, spicy, fruity and eggy
c) sweet, sour, bitter, salty and savoury
d) sweet, sour, salty, spicy and ewwwww

3. Where are your body's main balance organs found?

a) in your feet
b) in your knees
c) in your eyes
d) in your ears

>>>>>>>>>>>>>>>>>>>>>>>>>>>>

4. Which nerve carries information from the eye to the brain?

a) eyeball nerve
b) optic nerve
c) orbital nerve
d) auditory nerve

5. Which of the following is NOT a part of the eye?

a) pupil
b) iris
c) cochlea
d) retina

6. Why is there a 'blind spot' in every human eye?

a) because our noses block our vision
b) because our eyelids don't open wide enough
c) because our pupils don't open wide enough
d) because our retinas have holes in them

7. As people get older, they tend to get more:

a) near- (or short-)sighted
b) far- (or long-)sighted
c) colourblind
d) night-blind

8. How many other senses – in addition to sight, sound, smell, taste and touch – do humans have?

a) one
b) three
c) five
d) fifteen or more

9. What would be the result of damaging an auditory nerve?

a) blindness
b) deafness
c) inability to smell
d) inability to move

10. What are the two kinds of light receptor found in the human eye called?

a) cubes and cones
b) rods and cones
c) posts and pixels
d) eyeballs and eyebuds

B: PICTURE PUZZLE 1

Biggest Brains

Place these four animals in order of brain size (smallest first):

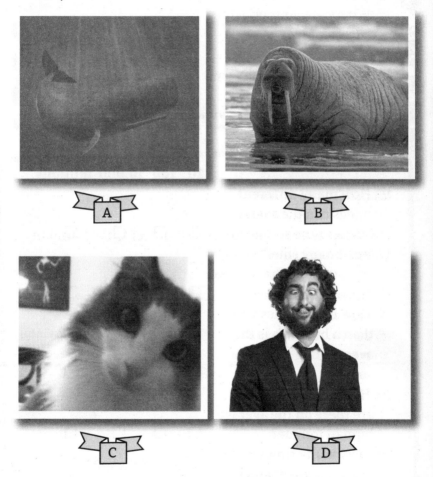

A

B

C

D

C: QUICK-FIRE QUESTIONS

	Eye	Ear	Nose	Mouth
11. Where would you find your tympanic membrane?	☐	☐	☐	☐
12. Where are your olfactory cells located?	☐	☐	☐	☐
13. Where are your corneas?	☐	☐	☐	☐
14. Where are your salivary glands found?	☐	☐	☐	☐
15. Whereabouts is your uvula?	☐	☐	☐	☐

	10	100	10,000	millions
16. How many different smells can the average human nose recognize?	☐	☐	☐	☐
17. How many smell receptors are there in the average human nose?	☐	☐	☐	☐
18. How many times better than a human's is the average dog's sense of smell?	☐	☐	☐	☐
19. How many taste buds are there on the average human tongue?	☐	☐	☐	☐
20. How many times better is your sense of smell, compared to taste?	☐	☐	☐	☐

	3	10	20	80
21. How much of the brain (in %) is made of water?	☐	☐	☐	☐
22. How much of your oxygen (in %) does your brain consume?	☐	☐	☐	☐
23. How much of your total blood flow (in %) does your brain use?	☐	☐	☐	☐
24. How long (in seconds) does the average dream last?	☐	☐	☐	☐
25. How much of our brains (in %) do we typically use at once?	☐	☐	☐	☐

	100	200	600	1,300
26. How heavy, in grams, is the average human brain?	☐	☐	☐	☐
27. How many miles of nerves run through your body?	☐	☐	☐	☐
28. How many billion cells does the average brain contain?	☐	☐	☐	☐
29. About how fast, in miles per hour, can a rapid nerve signal travel?	☐	☐	☐	☐
30. How many times better than ours is a cat's sense of smell?	☐	☐	☐	☐

D: PICTURE PUZZLE 2

Odd one out

Which one doesn't belong here, and why?

A

B

C

D

E: MORE MEGA-BRAIN QUESTIONS

31. Which half of your brain controls the left side of your body?

a) the left half
b) the right half
c) the front half
d) the back half

32. What type of nerve (or neuron) sends signals from the brain to the muscles?

a) muscle neuron
b) movement neuron
c) motor neuron
d) sensory neuron

33. How long could you survive with only half a brain?

a) 10 seconds
b) 10 minutes
c) 10 years
d) a lifetime

34. What makes humans smarter than all other mammals?

a) we have bigger heads
b) we have bigger brains
c) we have bigger forebrains
d) we have two brains

35. What lies between the brain and the skull?

a) nothing
b) membranes
c) watery goo
d) both (b) and (c)

36. Why are our brains all wrinkled on the outside?

a) the wrinkles protect and cushion the brain
b) the wrinkles shorten the connections between
   different parts of the brain
c) because our brains age faster than the rest of our
   bodies
d) because we evolved from cauliflowers

37. Why do we sleep?

a) to put the brain on 'standby' mode
b) to let the brain repair itself
c) to let the brain store memories from the day just gone
d) all of the above

38. What causes 'brain freeze' (aka 'ice-cream headache')?

a) altered blood flow to the brain
b) too much sugar entering the brain
c) too much fat entering the brain
d) the brain shrinks when it gets cold

39. How long can your brain survive without oxygen?

a) 1–2 minutes
b) 5–10 minutes
c) 10–20 minutes
d) up to an hour

40. Roughly speaking, how many thoughts does the average person have per day?

a) up to 100
b) up to 1,000
c) up to 10,000
d) up to 100,000

SENSORY PUZZLER

Use the clues to complete this brain-powered puzzle.

Across

4) Automatic reaction, controlled by nerves (6)

5) Nerve that carries signals from the eyes to the brain (5)

8) Wrinkled outer surface of the brain (6)

9) What motor neurons send signals to (7)

10) One of the five basic tastes your tongue can detect (5)

Down

1) What your vestibular organs help you sense and control (7)

2) Halves of the brain (11)

3) Another word for 'nerve cell' (6)

6) Shell-like organ of the inner ear (7)

7) Coloured muscular part of the eye (4)

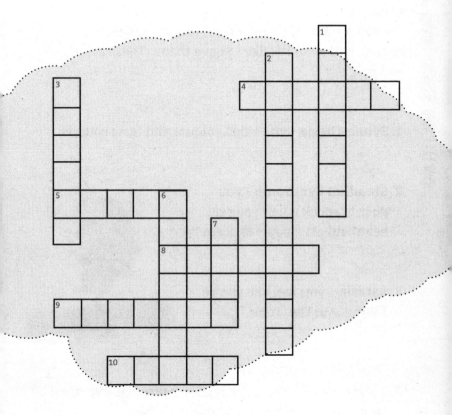

TOP 10 STRANGE BRAIN CONDITIONS

Weird things can happen when the brain is wired wrong or damaged.

Here are ten of the strangest brain conditions known, and what it's like to have them. (These are all real.)

1. **Synaesthesia** – you smell colours and taste sounds.

2. **Stendhal Syndrome** – you go into shock when you see beautiful art, people or scenery.

3. **Astasia** – you feel like you're falling. All. The. Time.

4. **Aphasia** – you can listen, read, write and understand language, but you lose the ability to speak.

5. **Foreign Accent Syndrome** – you can speak just fine. But you speak your own language with a foreign (e.g. French, Spanish, Russian) accent.

6. **Amelodia** – you can hear and play music, but you can't recognize tunes.

7. **Micropsia** – everything (from cars to pet cats) looks tiny and shrunken.

8. **Triskalidekaphobia** – you become inexplicably terrified of the number 13.

9. **Exploding Head Syndrome** – randomly and without warning, you hear a huge roaring sound in your head, which sounds like a massive explosion.

10. **Cotard's Syndrome (aka Zombie Syndrome)** – you believe yourself to be immortal or undead.

QUESTIONS

PART THREE: EARTHQUAKES, VOLCANOES AND NATURAL DISASTERS ⚡

Do you know what a *tsunami* is? How *tornadoes* are measured? How *avalanches* are triggered, and how fast they can tumble?

Get your wellies on – there's some nasty weather ahead . . .

Answers start on page 127.

SUPERGEEK: QUESTIONS

>>>>>>>>>>>>>>>>>>>>>>>>>>>>>>>

A: MEGA-BRAIN QUESTIONS

1. Where is the largest volcano in the world?

a) Japan
b) New Zealand
c) the Philippines
d) USA

2. What does a seismometer measure?

a) wind speeds
b) earthquakes
c) air pressures
d) the size of a tsunami wave

3. What do you call a scientist who studies volcanoes?

a) a vulcanologist
b) a pyrologist
c) a flammologist
d) a mentalist

>>>>>>>>>>>>>>>>>>>>>>>>>>>>

4. What's the difference between lava and magma?

a) lava is hot, magma isn't
b) lava flows, magma doesn't
c) lava flows above ground, magma flows below ground
d) lava is a liquid, magma is a solid

5. Which country has the most volcanoes?

a) USA
b) Italy
c) India
d) Indonesia

6. Why do earthquakes and tsunamis (tidal waves) often happen together?

a) because earthquakes cause tsunamis
b) because tsunamis cause earthquakes
c) because tsunamis are drawn to earthquakes
d) they don't – it just seems that way

7. What's the difference between a hurricane and a typhoon?

a) hurricanes are more powerful
b) typhoons are more powerful
c) they happen at different times of year
d) they're born from different oceans

8. What do hurricanes bring that makes them so dangerous and destructive?

a) strong winds
b) heavy rains
c) surging waves
d) all of the above

9. On which continents do tornadoes happen?

a) North America and South America
b) North America and Asia
c) North America and Africa
d) all but one of them

10. What is the name of the scale used to measure the size and power of a tornado?

a) the Beaufort scale
b) the Fujita scale
c) the Richter scale
d) the Twister scale

Dead or alive?

Which of these volcanoes are dead (extinct), and which are alive (or active?)

Arthur's Seat, Scotland

Mount Etna, Italy

Sakura-jima, Japan

Fuerteventura,
Canary Islands

C: QUICK-FIRE QUESTIONS

	60	100	300	900
11. How many of the world's volcanoes are active?	☐	☐	☐	☐
12. How many volcanoes dot the landscape of Chile?	☐	☐	☐	☐
13. How many active volcanoes are there in the fiery Philippines?	☐	☐	☐	☐
14. How many active volcanoes are there in Europe?	☐	☐	☐	☐
15. How many active volcanoes are there in Japan?	☐	☐	☐	☐

	2004	2005	2010	2011
16. In what year did Hurricane Katrina flood the city of New Orleans?	☐	☐	☐	☐
17. In what year did a tsunami devastate Indonesia and Sri Lanka?	☐	☐	☐	☐
18. When did the great Tohoku earthquake (and tsunami) hit Japan?	☐	☐	☐	☐
19. When did a massive earthquake cripple the Caribbean island of Haiti?	☐	☐	☐	☐
20. In what year did a rare tornado rip through Birmingham, England?	☐	☐	☐	☐

	Asia	Africa	Europe	USA
21. Where is the earthquake-prone San Andreas fault line?	☐	☐	☐	☐
22. Where do tsunami most commonly strike?	☐	☐	☐	☐
23. Which region is most often devastated by drought and famine?	☐	☐	☐	☐
24. Which region is most prone to dangerous tornadoes?	☐	☐	☐	☐
25. Which region is, on average, the least prone to natural disasters?	☐	☐	☐	☐

	35	74	200	450
26. How fast (in mph) must the winds be in a blizzard?	☐	☐	☐	☐
27. At what wind speed (in mph) does a storm become a hurricane?	☐	☐	☐	☐
28. How fast can the snow in an avalanche tumble?	☐	☐	☐	☐
29. How fast is the pyroclastic gas cloud that erupts from a volcano?	☐	☐	☐	☐
30. How fast are the winds within an F4 tornado?	☐	☐	☐	☐

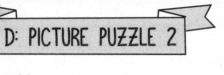

D: PICTURE PUZZLE 2

Odd one out

Which one doesn't belong here, and why?

A

Mount Fuji, Japan

B

Mount Everest, Nepal

C

Mount St Helens, USA

D

Mount Kilimanjaro,
Tanzania

E: MORE MEGA-BRAIN QUESTIONS

31. Name the Icelandic volcano that erupted in 2010, grounding European air traffic for almost a week?

a) Krafla
b) Eyjafjallajökull
c) Rekyahols
d) Björksgob

32. What triggers over 90% of all recorded avalanches?

a) fresh snowfall
b) sunny days
c) mountain goats
d) people

33. How much can a large avalanche weigh?

a) 10 tonnes
b) 100 tonnes
c) 1,000 tonnes
d) 10,000,000 tonnes

34. On average, which country sees the most deadly avalanches each year?

a) France
b) Switzerland
c) Norway
d) Canada

35. On which continent did over 35,000 people perish in a month-long heatwave in 2003?

a) Africa
b) Asia
c) Europe
d) Australia

36. What natural disaster flattened over 1,200 square miles of Siberian forest in 1905?

a) tidal wave
b) typhoon
c) volcanic eruption
d) exploding asteroid

37. How wide was the object that created the 100-mile wide Chicxulub crater in Mexico?

a) 10m
b) 1km
c) 10km
d) 100km

38. How wide would an asteroid have to be to wipe out all human life on the planet?

a) 10m
b) 1km
c) 10km
d) 100km

39. What is special about the African 'crater lakes' Nyos, Monoun and Kivu?

a) they're made of acid
b) they're made of lava
c) they spew deadly fumes
d) both (a) and (c)

40. How tall was the largest tidal wave in recorded history?

a) 50m (165 feet)
b) 100m (330 feet)
c) 500m (1,640 feet)
d) 1,000m (3,280 feet)

DISASTER PUZZLER

Use the clues to solve this natural-disaster-themed crossword

Across
4) Violent snowstorm (8)
6) Spinning wind funnel, also known as a 'twister' (7)
7) Uncontrolled wilderness fire, often started by a lightning strike during a dry season (also known as a forest fire, brush fire or bush fire) (8)
8) Dangerous snowslide (9)
10) Hurricane that flooded the city of New Orleans, USA, in 2005 (7)

Down
1) Tidal wave (7)
2) Scale used to measure the strength of earthquakes (7)
3) Volcanic island between Java and Sumatra, which erupted in 1883, making a bang that was heard over 3,000 miles away (8)
5) Name given to a quiet or 'sleeping' volcano (7)
9) Volcano that erupted in AD 79, burying the Italian town of Pompeii in ash (8)

TOP 10 ILL-ADVISED EXTREME SPORTS

1. Wakeboarding (during a tsunami)

2. Windsurfing (into a typhoon)

3. Hang-gliding (into a hurricane)

4. Free running (during an earthquake)

5. Abseiling (into an active volcano)

6. Tobogganing (atop an avalanche)

7. Rock climbing (during a sandstorm)

8. Ice climbing (during a blizzard)

9. Bungee jumping (during a tornado)

10. Anything (during an asteroid impact)

QUESTIONS

PART FOUR: PLANES, TRAINS AND TRANSPORT 🚀

Do you know how oil tankers stay afloat? How submarines sink? What a *MagLev* train is? What makes the Volkswagen *Aqua* so special?

Let's shift into high gear for the fourth and final chapter!

Answers start on page 157.

SUPERGEEK: QUESTIONS

>>>>>>>>>>>>>>>>>>>>>>>>>>>>>>

A: MEGA-BRAIN QUESTIONS

1. What do aeroplanes have that gliders lack?

a) wings
b) tails
c) pilots
d) engines

2. What force keeps aeroplanes in the air?

a) gravity
b) lift
c) thrust
d) magic

3. Why can't most aeroplanes fly into space?

a) because their engines don't work in space
b) because their wings don't work in space
c) because they're not airtight, so all the passengers
   would suffocate
d) they could, they're just not allowed

4. All aeroplanes can rotate in three planes (or directions). What do pilots call these?

a) pitch, turn and bank
b) pitch, turn and roll
c) pitch, yaw and roll
d) up, up and away

5. Why do airliners follow curved (rather than straight) paths across the Atlantic?

a) because they're following the curve of the Earth
b) because they're trying to avoid planes coming the other way
c) because the wind blows them off-course
d) because their GPS navigation systems are rubbish

6. What's so special about a MagLev train?

a) it's the biggest and longest in the world
b) it tilts as it goes around corners
c) it floats above the track
d) it needs no rails or tracks

7. In which country is the world's fastest passenger train line?

a) Japan
b) China
c) Germany
d) USA

8. How long was the longest ship ever built?

a) 100m (328 feet) – the size of two Olympic swimming
   pools
b) 317m (1,040 feet) – the size of London's Wembley
   Stadium
c) 460m (1,500 feet) – the size of New York's Empire
   State Building
d) 828m (2,716 feet) – the size of the Burj Khalifah
   tower in Dubai

9. How do massive oil tankers stay afloat?

a) they are made entirely of lightweight materials
b) oil is lighter than air
c) they have helium balloons attached to their hulls
d) they weigh less than the amount of water they push
   aside

10. What happens when a submarine fills its ballast tanks with air?

a) it sinks
b) it rises
c) it fires a torpedo
d) nothing

What is it?

Name the famous aircraft in each of these pictures:

A

B

C

D

C: QUICK-FIRE QUESTIONS

	375	400	650	850
11. How heavy (in tonnes) is a standard Boeing 747 airliner?	☐	☐	☐	☐
12. How heavy is an Airbus A380 Superjumbo airliner?	☐	☐	☐	☐
13. How many passengers can fit inside an A380?	☐	☐	☐	☐
14. What's the top speed (in mph) of an A380?	☐	☐	☐	☐
15. How much (in millions of US dollars) does one A380 cost?	☐	☐	☐	☐

	1880s	1900s	1930s	1940s
16. In which decade was the first working helicopter built and flown?	☐	☐	☐	☐
17. When did the *Hindenberg* airship famously catch fire and crash?	☐	☐	☐	☐
18. When was the jet engine invented?	☐	☐	☐	☐
19. In which decade was the world's first powered flight?	☐	☐	☐	☐
20. When was the world's first supersonic flight?	☐	☐	☐	☐

	167	318	456	763
21. How fast (in mph) is *Thrust SSC*, the world's fastest supersonic car?	☐	☐	☐	☐
22. What's the highest speed (in mph) ever reached by a railed train?	☐	☐	☐	☐
23. How fast (in mph) can a Japanese 'bullet' train take corners?	☐	☐	☐	☐
24. What's the speed record (in mph) for a boat?	☐	☐	☐	☐
25. What's the highest speed (in mph) ever reached (on flat ground) on a bicycle?	☐	☐	☐	☐

	2	6	8	12
26. How many seconds did the Wright brothers' first flight last?	☐	☐	☐	☐
27. How many minutes does it take to launch a Space Shuttle into orbit?	☐	☐	☐	☐
28. A typical Formula One racing car can go from 0 to 60 mph in how many seconds?	☐	☐	☐	☐
29. How many rotor blades are there on a standard Bell (or 'Huey') helicopter?	☐	☐	☐	☐
30. How many rotor blades are there on a twin-engined Chinook?	☐	☐	☐	☐

D: PICTURE PUZZLE 2

Odd one out

Which one doesn't belong here, and why?

A
Hovercraft

B
Ground-Effect Train

C
MagLev Train

D
Hydrofoil

E: MORE MEGA-BRAIN QUESTIONS

31. What do the Nissan Leaf, the Opel Ampera and the Tesla Roadster all have in common?

a) they're all electric cars
b) they're all hybrid cars
c) they all run on ethanol fuel
d) they all run on hydrogen fuel

32. Which two parts provide the power for most Hybrid Electric Vehicles ?

a) petrol engine and diesel engine
b) petrol engine and hydrogen fuel cell
c) petrol engine and electric motor
d) petrol engine and nuclear reactor

33. All Formula 1 cars have spoilers. What does a spoiler do?

a) it decreases drag and air resistance
b) it increases the car's grip on the road
c) it protects the back wheels during crashes
d) it just makes the car look cooler

34. What was special about *Stanley*, the car that won the DARPA Grand Challenge race in 2005?

a) it was solar-powered
b) it was hydrogen-powered
c) it had no wheels
d) it had no driver

35. What can the Terrafugia Transition do that most cars cannot?

a) float
b) fly
c) turn invisible
d) transform into a giant robot

36. When was the first Space Shuttle mission?

a) 1981
b) 1991
c) 2001
d) 2011

37. Which of the following was *not* part of NASA's Space Shuttle fleet?

a) *Atlantis*
b) *Intrepid*
c) *Endeavour*
d) *Enterprise*

38. What is the maximum speed reached by a Space Shuttle in orbit?

a) 175 mph
b) 1,750 mph
c) 17,500 mph
d) 175,000 mph

39. What makes spacecraft 'burn up' as they re-enter the atmosphere?

a) friction
b) solar radiation
c) the Earth's magnetic field
d) global warming

40. What is the name of the world's first private passenger spacecraft, launched in 2004?

a) *Sirius*
b) *StarCab*
c) *SpaceCruiser*
d) *SpaceShipOne*

SPEEDY PUZZLER

Use the clues to complete this tricky transport-themed crossword.

Across

3) Type of car with both a petrol engine and an electric motor (6)

5) Japanese 'Bullet Train' – one of the world's fastest passenger trains (10)

7) What keeps a MagLev train hovering above its tracks (14)

9) High-speed amphibious vehicle that floats on a cushion of air (10)

Down

1) Force that prevents the tyres of a racing car from leaving the track during a fast turn (8)

2) Force that keeps ships and other watercraft afloat (8)

4) Type of high-speed aircraft engine invented by British engineer Frank Whittle in 1937 (3)

5) Name given to an aeroplane (e.g. the Space Shuttle) that can also fly in space (10)

6) Force that slows an aircraft or racing car, due to air resistance (4)

8) Movable control surface used to steer an aircraft or ship (6)

TOP 10 COOLEST. CARS. EVER.

Some of these have been built, others only designed.
But one thing's for sure – they are all awesome.

1. **A360**. Runs on three spheres, rather than wheels.
   Can roll in any direction, and the cabin swivels 360°
   so that the driver is always facing forward.

2. **Peugeot Globule**. Shapeshifting car that consists of
   four separate blobs or modules – each with its own
   motor and seat. By shifting the modules around, you
   can drive two-in-front, two-behind, or all in a line –
   like a big, rolling caterpillar.

3. **BMW Gina**. A super-sleek BMW roadster covered with
   a metallic fabric 'skin' to make it look and feel like
   a living thing. Oh, and its headlights have blinking
   eyelids.

4. **Peugeot Ozone**. Like a two-seater sofa in a hamster ball. (The electric engine is underneath, in case you were wondering.)

5. **Kazaguruma** (Japanese for 'Windmobile'). Wind-powered buggy that drives itself by redirecting wind-flow across a set of tail-mounted fan blades.

6. **Foow**. Solar-powered three-wheeler which tilts upright so you can park it in tighter spaces.

7. **P-Eco**. Piezoelectric car with a battery strung through with metallic 'chords' that convert movement into electricity. In short, an electric car that charges its own battery as it moves.

8. **Volkswagen Aqua**. Yeah, that's right. It's a combination car–hovercraft, which skims across the waves almost as well as it rolls over flat terrain. James Bond, eat your heart out.

9. **Fiat Eye**. A one-seater electric city car with two ovoid wheels and a cabin that swings and balances like a rocking cradle. And it's entirely voice-controlled! Shout 'home', and its eggy wheels will start a-rollin' . . .

10. **Honda Native**. Sleek aerodynamic wedge with an ecofriendly electric motor. Not impressed? Well get this – it also changes colour to match your house, your lawn or your clothes. In short, it's a chameleon car.

ANSWERS

PART ONE: DINOSAURS AND PREHISTORIC LIFE

SUPERGEEK: ANSWERS

>>>>>>>>>>>>>>>>>>>>>>>>>>>>

A: MEGA-BRAIN ANSWERS

1. (a) Stegosaurus
The name 'stegosaurus' means
'roofed lizard' – a
reference to the set
of triangular tiles or
plates found alongside most
stegosaurus skeletons. Although scientists know that
every stegosaurus had these, what we don't exactly
know is *why* they had them. Some palaeontologists
believe they were for self-defence – a row of spiked
plates to discourage bites from tall carnivores. Others
think the plates might have been there to attract
females, as antlers do for modern-day stags. And still
others say the plates were used to help stegosaurus cool
off, by increasing the surface area of its body.

Nor are we sure *how the plates were arranged* on the
animal's back. Some believe the plates would lie flat, all
along the animal's back, forming an interlocking bony
'zip' that protected the delicate spine beneath. But most
palaeontologists seem to think they were arranged in
two rows either side of the spine, with the pointy ends
jutting upward towards the sky.

Stegosaurus, they say, might not have been
too bright. But it certainly had style!

>>>>>>>>>>>>>>>>>>>>>>>>>>>>>>

2. (c) three

The name 'triceratops' means 'three-horned'.

Bit of a giveaway, that. However, palaeontologists are still arguing over whether Triceratops is one species, several species, or not a species at all.

In fact, you could argue that the name '**tri**ceratops' is a bit misleading, since the animal only had two genuine, bull-like horns on its head. In an adult *Triceratops*, these could reach up to 1m (3 feet) in length. The third 'horn' was much stubbier, and stuck on to the animal's snout, like that of a rhino. Inside, this one was made of a different material to the other two. But since all three were covered in tough **keratin** protein (the same stuff human hair and rhino horns are made of), in effect, *Triceratops* had three horns.

That said, *Triceratops* was part of a larger family of animals called Ceratopsids, which included species with more – or fewer – horns.

Toroceratops ('bull horns') lacked a snout horn, so had just two horns on its head.

Pentaceratops had five horns.

Diabloceratops ('devil horns') had three horns on its head and snout, a pair of spikes sticking out of its jaws, and two long spikes jutting straight up from its bony frill. How cool is *that*?

3. (d) to warm up, *and* to attract females

Dimetrodons, or sailback lizards, were *not* dinosaurs. They were *Pelycosaurs*: large, tiger-sized reptiles that lived during the Permian era, around 50 million years before the first dinosaurs evolved. The first *Dimetrodon* fossil was found in the late 1800s,

and the animal gets its name from the two types of teeth found in its skull. 'Dimetrodon' means 'two-length teeth'. But its most obvious and spectacular feature is the enormous sail on its back.

The sail was formed by a row of fence-like spines – each sticking out of the animal's own backbone – with a layer of skin stretched between. For decades, palaeontologists argued about why the sail was there, and how *Dimetrodon* used it. It seems likely that the sail, which increased the animal's skin surface by 50%, helped the cold-blooded reptile to warm up quickly in the early-morning sun. Crocodiles and alligators still bask in the sun to warm up today. And anything that might have helped *Dimetrodon* warm up faster, and catch more prey, might have helped it survive better in the Permian world.

It also seems likely, though, that male *Dimetrodons* used their *sails* the same way peacocks use their *tails* – to attract females. Beyond a certain size, the sails probably didn't help that much with warming up, and became more of a hindrance to the animal than a help. But because **female Dimetrodons kept choosing males with the tallest sails**, the sails grew bigger and bigger with each generation. In short, **the ladies liked a large sail on their male**. And in biology, what the lady **wants**, the lady **gets**.

4. (b) a huge prehistoric shark

Megalodon (meaning 'massive teeth') was a species of shark which first appeared around 28 million years ago, over 30 million years after most of the dinosaurs had died out. Thankfully – at least for swimmers and surfers – *Megalodon* eventually died out too, around 1.5 million years ago. I say this because **Megalodon was HUGE**. Adults measured up to 20m (60 feet) long –

roughly **twice** the size of modern-day **whale sharks,** and nearly **four times** the size of the dreaded **great white shark.**

It had **hundreds** of teeth,

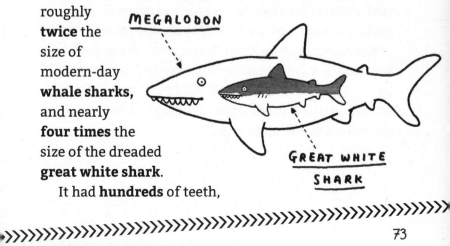

MEGALODON

GREAT WHITE SHARK

arranged in 3–5 rows that spanned its huge jaws. Each measured over 18cm (7 inches) long – roughly the size of a large kitchen knife. It also had the strongest bite of any known animal. It could crush a whale's skull or a giant turtle's shell in one bite. If it was still around today, it would be swallowing scuba divers whole and biting through the hulls of small boats to get at passengers.

Good thing it's *not*, then.

5. (c) awesome lizard

It's often said that *dinosaur* means 'terrible lizard' or 'fearsome lizard'. This is true.

Dino- comes from the Greek word *deinos*, meaning 'terrible' or 'fearsome', and *-saur* from *sauros*, meaning 'lizard'. But when palaeontologist Richard Owen gave the Dinosauria family its name back in 1842, he wasn't referring to their scary teeth, claws and horns. In fact, he didn't mean 'terrible' in the sense of 'scary' or 'terrifying' at all. The *real* meaning of *deinos* is closer to 'terribly great', 'awe-inspiring' or simply 'AWESOME'.

Among all the lizard families known to science at that time, the dinosaurs were the largest, the greatest, the most impressive. So Owen dubbed them 'awesome lizards'. And who could argue with that? After all, dinosaurs *are* awesome, right?

6. (d) fly

The old, nineteenth-century view of dinosaurs was that they were slow, lumbering beasts. And while some of them (like *Brachiosaurus*) might well have been slow plodders, most were active, fast-moving reptiles. Plenty of dinosaurs could run and jump. Ornithomimids (literally, 'ostrich-mimics') like *Dromiceiomimus* could sprint at **60km (35 miles) per hour** or more.

Velociraptors – speedy animals in their own right – could leap **3 metres (10 feet)** or more straight up, using their powerful hind legs. Other lightweight therapods might have been just as agile, or even more so.

ON YOUR MARKS! GET SET!

There's evidence that many therapod dinosaurs could **swim** too. This is, perhaps, not surprising, given that so much of our planet's surface is covered by rivers, lakes, seas and oceans. It's hard to see how dinosaurs could have ruled the Earth for over 120 million years without being able to paddle once in a while.

It wasn't just the *little* ones that swam either. In 2007, scientists in Spain found scratch marks in a Cretaceous-period river bed, made by an adult *Tyrannosaurus* doggy-paddling its way across. Imagine seeing *that* swimming towards you at the local pool.

But for all their running, jumping and paddling, **no known dinosaur could actually fly.** Pterosaurs (including the famous *Pterodacytls*) could fly, of course. **But they weren't dinosaurs.**

Weren't they? They were flying reptiles that lived *alongside* (or rather, above) the dinosaurs, during the same time period. Many feathered, bird-like dinosaurs evolved during the Jurassic age, and some could probably glide short distances between trees (like flying squirrels do today) or add height to their jumps by flapping. But most had bones that were too **dense** and **heavy** to allow even that.

Archaeopteryx was the first known therapod with bones light enough to fly. But since it could fly, it is classified as the first known bird, rather than a rare flying dinosaur. By the Cretaceous age, flying therapods (i.e. birds) dominated the skies. But by then they had a new name, and their own class, separate from their reptilian ancestors. So strictly speaking, dinosaurs did not fly. Rather, some of them evolved into birds, which *could*.

7. (a) plants

When most people hear the word 'dinosaur', they think 'dangerous carnivore', or more often, '*T. Rex*'. But in fact, **only about a third of all known dinosaur species were meat-eaters. The other two-thirds were herbivores, or plant-eaters.**

From a biologist's viewpoint, this makes perfect sense. Like animals today, the dinosaurs formed food chains in their local environments – with plants at the bottom, plant-eaters in the middle, and carnivores (i.e. plant-eater-eaters) at the top.

A good rule of thumb for food chains is that each species in the chain is supported by at least 10 times as much food or prey (animals or plants further down the chain) to survive. So 1,000 plants would support roughly 100 herbivores, which in turn would support 10 large carnivores. If you don't have enough herbivores, the carnivores simply cannot survive. Not everybody, it seems, gets to be a *T. Rex*.

This might also help explain why the largest dinosaurs began dying out even before the deadly meteorite impact of 65 million years ago. The climate, it seems, was already changing, and large herbivores were unable to adapt quickly enough to survive. With fewer large herbivores around, the large carnivores began dying off too. When the meteorite struck, it blocked out the sun for years, gradually killing off many of the plant species the remaining herbivores relied upon. This, in time, killed off almost everything further up the chain. More's the pity.

8. (d) Spinosaurus

All of these animals were large meat-eating **therapod** dinosaurs, and you wouldn't want to meet *any* of them on a dark night. Or any time of day, for that matter. They all walked upright on two powerful hind legs, and while they probably weren't the smartest of the carnivores, they were fast, powerful and agile enough to make lunch out of anything smaller or slower than themselves. Some even brought down lumbering herbivores that were *bigger* than they were.

Allosaurus measured up to **7.5m (25 feet) long**, stood over **3m (10 feet) tall**, and fed on (among other things) largish herbivores like *Stegosaurus*. Adult *Tyrannosaurs* (including the famous *T. Rex*) were over **13m (43 feet) long**, **5m (16 feet) tall**, weighed 9 tonnes, and could crush the bones of a Sauropod with its massive, powerful jaws. But while *T. Rex* is probably the

best-known therapod dinosaur, it certainly wasn't the biggest. Or the meanest.

The **average** *Gigantosaurus* was about the same length, height and weight as the largest known *T. Rex*, and had an even *larger* shark-like skull. But the biggest and baddest therapod discovered so far is Spinosaurus. A good **3m (10 feet) longer** than *T. Rex*, and **3 tonnes heavier**, this bad boy could eat your average Tyrannosaur for breakfast in a straight fight. Its massive crocodilian snout probably evolved to catch large fish in shallow water. But it was equally happy chowing down on anything else that got in its way – including the largest of its dinosaur cousins.

9. (c) tiny thick-headed lizard

Dinosaurs are rarely given random names. Most often, their names are made up of ancient Greek or Latin words that describe their features, or where they were found. If you're interested in dinosaurs, it's worth learning a few words in Greek so that you can understand and remember their names better.

Often the name includes a body part, or it could describe the size or shape of an animal (or one of its body parts).

Cephalo- means 'head',

Ptero- means 'wing', and

-don means 'tooth'. It might also describe the size or
      shape of an animal (or one of its body parts).

Here, *Megalo-* means 'huge',

Micro- means 'tiny',

Platy- means 'flat' and

Pachy- means 'thick'.

Hence, *Pterosaur* means 'winged lizard',

pachycephalosaurus means 'thick-headed lizard'
and

Micropachycephalosaurus means 'tiny thick-headed lizard'.

Simple, eh?

10. (b) Pterosaurs

Pterosaurs (meaning 'winged lizards') are often mistakenly called *Pterodactyls* in books and movies. *Pterodactylus* (meaning 'wing finger') got its name from having wings that stretched between its body to its (freakishy long) little fingers. It was a smallish animal, with a wingspan of just **1 metre (3 feet)**. But *Pterodactylus* was just one species group within a larger family of prehistoric, flying lizards.

Other Pterosaurs included the small, fish-hunting *Dimorphodon*, and the larger, condor-like *Pteranodon* – which, with a wingspan of over 6 feet, was more than twice the size of *Pterodactylus*.

But even these looked like sparrows next to the monstrous *Quetzalcoatlus*. A giant Pterosaur of the Cretaceous age, the terrifying Quetzalcoatlus had a **12-metre (40-foot) wingspan**, weighed over **250kg (500lb)** and stood over **three times** taller than a man on land. This huge flying reptile was the size of a passenger aeroplane, and unlike other fish-eating Pterosaurs, it spent most of its time flying over land, hunting dinosaurs and other large prey. Let's be glad this flying nightmare isn't still up there, stalking *us*.

B: PICTURE PUZZLE 1

A – Triceratops

B – Plesiosaur

C – Ankylosaur

D – Spinosaur

C: QUICK-FIRE ANSWERS

11. **5 horns**.
12. **3cm**.
13. **1m tall**. Real *Velociraptors* were little bigger than geese. The species seen in the *Jurassic Park* movies was their much larger cousin, *Deinonychus*.
14. **2 feet**. All Therapods are bipeds.
15. **2m**. Although much larger Pterosaurs existed, Pterodactyls were pretty small.
16. **30 tonnes**.
17. **17** African elephants.
18. **13m tall**. The tallest *Sauropod*, Sauroposeidon, reached 18m or more.
19. **100 years**.
20. (Almost) **100 vertebrae**, or neck bones.
21. **50 tonnes**. *Seismosaurus* was among the heaviest of the Sauropods; hence its name, which means 'earthquake lizard'!
22. **100 tonnes** (over three times heavier than *Brachiosaurus*, and twice as heavy as *Seismosaurus*. That's a big lad!).
23. **30 years**. Energetic predators rarely live as long as lumbering grazers.
24. **50mph** (equivalent to modern-day ostriches).
25. **1,000**. Right now the number sits at around 950, but there are plenty more to be found!
26. **Most**. About **four-fifths** of all dinosaur fossils have been discovered by amateur fossil hunters, rather than professional scientists.

27. **Half** of all known dinosaur species were found within the last 20 years. Partly because we're getting better at finding them.
28. **Most** dinosaur species were small-ish bipeds, rather than huge, heavy quadrupeds.
29. **Most of them**. Dinosaur fossils have been found in 35 out of 50, so far.
30. **None**. Sadly. Birds are the **living descendants** of Therapod dinosaurs, but since they have their own class outside of the Reptiles, they cannot be classified as Dinosaurs.

D: PICTURE PUZZLE 2

C – **Tyrannosaurus**. It's the only true dinosaur of the bunch. The others – *Plesiosaurus*, *Dimetrodon* and *Pteranodon* – are all prehistoric reptiles, but not dinosaurs.

E: MORE MEGA-BRAIN ANSWERS

31. (b) Triassic

The first of the true dinosaurs evolved around 250 million years ago, during the Triassic age.

That said, they were by no means the first large, mean reptiles on the planet. During the Permian age, 50 million years earlier, **Archosaurs** and **Therapsids** – meat- and plant-eating reptiles that varied in size from mouse to monster – ruled the Earth. These included the sail-backed *Dimetrodon* and the dog-like *Cynognathus*.

Sadly, most of these died out during the **Permian Extinction** that killed off three-quarters of the animal species on the planet. This was probably caused by a supervolcano eruption that happened at the very end of the Permian period, around 252 million years ago. Had this extinction not happened, the dinosaurs might never have had their shot at ruling the world. In fact, for 20 million years after the Permian Extinction, most dinosaurs were little bigger than dogs or chickens, and monstrous prehistoric crocodiles topped the food chains, eating both dinosaurs and many of the surviving Archosaurs. It wasn't until about 200 million years ago, at the end of the Triassic age and the beginning of the Jurassic, that the dinosaurs grew in size, type and number, and eventually came to dominate the Earth.

300 million years ago	Permian age	Archosaurus and Therapsids ruled the world
250 million years ago	Triassic age	First dinosaurs evolved
200 million years ago	Jurassic age	Dinosaurs grew in size, type and number and dominated the Earth
145 million years ago	Cretaceous age	Dinosaurs reached their peak, and the first mammals evolved

32. (d) Cretaceous

Although the dinosaurs reached their peak during the Jurassic age, many of the best-known species – including *Triceratops* and *Tyrannosaurus rex* – were creatures of the Cretaceous period, which began around 145 million years ago. For a good 80 million years, these late-age dinosaurs stomped about, devouring all and enjoying total dominance over the prehistoric fish, amphibians and other reptiles attempting to survive in their midst. And although the first mammals also evolved during this period nothing larger than a mouse could survive with the dinosaurs still strong on the scene.

That is, until the end of the Cretaceous period, when a massive asteroid or comet impact triggered the downfall of the dinosaurs, and the rise of the mammals. This didn't happen all at once, however. Some dinosaur species (including *Triceratops*) struggled on for tens of thousands of years after the impact. And it took about as much time for mammals to grow and slip into the niches left behind by the disappearing dinos.

33. (d) all of the above
Turtles, crocodiles and insects all lived alongside the dinosaurs during the Jurassic and Cretaceous periods. In fact, there were **hundreds** more species of turtles and crocs than there are now, and **tens of thousands** more insect species. Some Jurassic turtle species were the size of small boats, and monster crocodiles grew to over 14m (45 feet) long – roughly the same size as an adult *Tyrannosaurus rex*.

The insects were larger too. With a thicker, more oxygen-rich atmosphere, some giant Jurassic dragonflies grew to the size of large birds, with wingspans of up to 70cm (30 inches) or more.

34. (c) a palaeontologist
'Palaeontologist' is the name given to a scientist who studies all forms of prehistoric life (including dinosaurs and prehistoric reptiles). For the most part,

CoooL!

they use fossils and other types of geological evidence to deduce how extinct prehistoric animals lived, evolved and interacted.

Palaeobotanists study prehistoric **plants**, rather than animals, and **herpetologists** study modern (i.e. living) reptiles and amphibians.

More recently, a new field of science called **palaeobiology** has emerged.

Palaeobiologists also study dinosaurs and prehistoric life. But they do so by combing evidence from fossils with knowledge from modern biology and living animal species. This includes studying proteins and DNA to figure out the relationships between living and long-dead species.

35. (b) the size of a car

The smallest known dinosaur was about the size of a dormouse. The largest was the size of five double-decker buses. Most dinosaurs, though, were neither tiny nor enormous. Speedy, chicken-sized Therapods were common. As were large, lumbering, rhino-like quadrupeds. On balance, this made the average size for a dinosaur about 4m (13 feet) long and 1.5m (4 feet) tall – i.e. about the same size as a family car.

36. (b) North America

More dinosaur species have been discovered in North America than anywhere else on Earth – partly as a result of its sheer area, and partly because the climate and geology there have produced more well-preserved fossils in general. That said, China comes in a close second and is catching up fast.

Topping the list of North America's dino-discovery 'hotspots' is **Alberta, Canada**, where tar sands have helped to preserve the 38+ species discovered in that state alone. In the USA, hotspots include **Montana**,

Wyoming, **Texas**, **Utah**, **Arizona** and **New Mexico**.
In Asia, the eastern Chinese province of **Shandong**
became a palaeontologist's dream when thousands of
Cretaceous-era fossils were unearthed there in 2008.
Mongolia too has been home to hundreds of dinosaur
discoveries.

Perhaps the world's first 'dinosaur hotspot' is
England's **Jurassic Coast**, which runs from coastal
Devon to **Dorset**. Although not dinosaurs, the first
known icthyosaurs and plesiosaurs were unearthed
there in the nineteenth century, and scores of complete
dinosaur skeletons have been found there – one as
recently as 2008.

37. (d) seven

Dinosaur fossils have been found on all seven of the world's major continents. As we've already seen, **North America** is positively teeming with dinosaur fossils, as are the **Asian** regions of China, Russia and Mongolia. In **Europe**, France, England and Germany have all been home to many finds. In **South America**, many unique fossils have been found in the Patagonia region of Argentina.

More species have been found in **South Africa**, the African island of Madagascar and the deserts of southwestern **Australia**. And believe it or not, several species of dinosaur were found beneath the ice sheets of **Antarctica**.

This might seem surprising, given the climate and layout of the continents today. But you have to remember

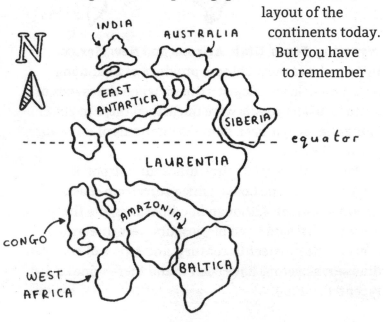

that in the time of the dinosaurs, the continents were still packed quite closely together, the warmer climate meant less ice and snow, and Antarctica formed a **land bridge** between the southern parts of Africa, Australia and South America. In fact, the finding of similar dinosaur fossils (in regions now located so far apart) gave twentieth-century geologists the clues they needed to figure out how the continents had shifted and moved over time.

38. (b) the size of a walnut

Stegosaurs weighed over four tonnes, were over 9m (30 feet) long and, including its spiny back-plates, stood over 3m (10 feet) tall. But its tiny brain measured no more than a few centimetres across – roughly the size of a walnut. Needless to say, it probably wasn't the smartest tool in the box. Then again, the brain of most **dogs** isn't much larger, and they seem smart enough. Think of it like a huge, dopey, heavily armoured puppy, and you probably won't be too far off the mark.

A WALNUT

TINY BRAIN!

39. (c) Dimetrodons

While *Hadrosaurs* and several species of *Ceratopsid* (including *Triceratops*) roamed the Cretaceous Earth alongside *T. Rex*, Dimetrodons died out at the end of the Permian age, over 100 million years earlier. So they could never have formed part of its diet.

Tyrannosaur bite marks on the leg bones of **other** Tyrannosaurs have led some palaeontologists to believe that *T. Rex* was a cannibal. Like modern-day lions, it probably killed other species for the most part. But if it found a dead cousin – or killed one in a battle for a mate or territory – it wasn't above scoffing down the corpse. In fact, some palaeontologists argue that *T. Rex* was more scavenger than hunter – more like a hyena than a lion. In reality, it was probably a little of both.

40. (b) sauropods

The tallest, longest and heaviest dinosaurs that ever existed were all members of the Sauropod family. Sauropods were huge plant-eating quadrupeds, which (like modern elephants) grew to immense sizes, and survived among predators chiefly by being **too huge to tackle**. Like giraffes, their long legs (and even longer necks) allowed them to graze on foliage well above the reach of rival herbivores, and the males might have swung their long necks at each other in battles over females.

The best-known Sauropods, *Brachiosaurus* and *Diplodocus*, weighed up to **30 tonnes**, grew up to **60m**

(200 feet) long and, with neck raised up, stood up to **9m (30 feet)** tall. But these weren't even the biggest of the bunch. *Seismosaurus* weighed **50 tonnes**, and might have stood up to **25m (85 feet)** tall at full stretch.

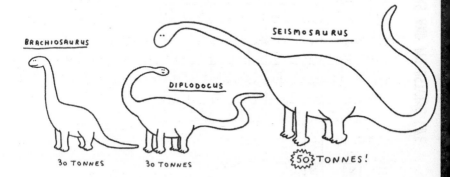

BRACHIOSAURUS

DIPLODOCUS

SEISMOSAURUS

30 TONNES

30 TONNES

50 TONNES!

Lankypods do not exist. I made them up. (But maybe if someone finds an even taller Sauropod, they'll consider using the name . . .)

PREHISTORIC PUZZLER SOLUTION

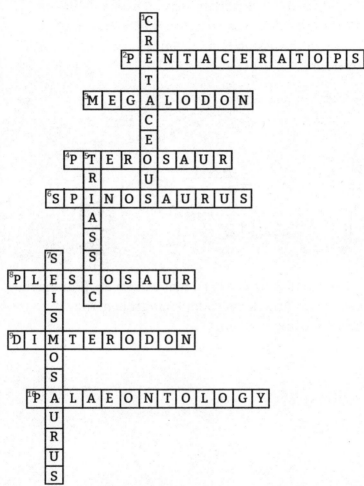

ANSWERS

PART TWO:
BRAINS, SENSES
AND FEELINGS

SUPERGEEK: ANSWERS

>>>>>>>>>>>>>>>>>>>>>>>>>>>>>>
A: MEGA-BRAIN ANSWERS

1. (b) reds and greens

When we say somebody is 'colourblind', it very rarely means they can't see any colours at all. There is a condition, called *monochromacy*, in which people are unable to see colours at all, and see only in shades of black, white and grey. But this is *extremely* rare (only 1 in every 100,000 people is born with it). Usually, being 'colourblind' means being unable to tell the difference between shades of red and green, something doctors call **anomalous trichromacy** or **red–green colourblindness**.

Around **1 in 20 boys** (but just **1 in 200 girls**) are born with red–green colourblindness. It's the result of damaged genes, which alter the shape of colour-sensing cone cells in the back of the eye. There are three types of cone cell in every eye – each one 'tuned' to pick up a certain *wavelength* (or colour) of light.

L cones sense **long (reddish) wavelengths**,

M cones sense **medium (greenish) wavelengths**, and

S cones sense **short (bluish) wavelengths**.

With all *three* types present and in good working order, you can tell the difference between **all** these colours, plus everything in between (yellows, purples, and so on).

But red–green colourblind people are born with slightly misshapen proteins in their L (**red**) and M (**green**) cone cells. So their 'red detectors' start picking up more greenish hues, and their 'green detectors' start picking up more reddish ones. As a result, they have trouble telling the difference between certain shades of red and green. In short, some (but not all) reds and greens look the same to them.

Blue–yellow colourblindness, caused by misshapen **S cone** proteins, also exists. But it is *much* rarer, affecting only **1 in 10,000** people (boys and girls in equal numbers).

2. (c) sweet, sour, bitter, salty and savoury

Tastes are picked up by **taste buds** on the tongue. These are the little bumps you see on your tongue when you poke it out in the mirror. Each taste bud, in turn, is covered with thousands of tiny **taste receptors** (a type of **chemoreceptor** protein). As foods and drinks – dissolved in saliva – wash over your tongue, the fats, salts, proteins and other chemicals within bind to these taste receptors and trigger a response.

There are hundreds of types of taste receptors, each one 'tuned' to recognize a different chemical. Once they have, they send a signal to the brain through nerves attached to each taste bud, telling it what combination of tastes the food or drink contains. This information, when compared with smell signals from the nose, combines in the brain to form the overall flavour of the food. But while there are thousands of **flavours** in the world, **tastes** are few.

For many years, scientists believed our tongues could detect only **four** basic tastes – **sweet, sour, bitter** and **salty**. Each of these tastes has a type of taste receptor associated with it. But recently, scientists in Japan discovered a **fifth** type of taste receptor on our tongues, which picks up a **fifth** taste they named *umami*.

This is Japanese for 'meaty' or 'savoury'. So the five basic tastes our tongues can pick up are sweet, sour, bitter, salty and savoury.

There's a reason, of course, for being able to taste each of these things. Toxic plants and poisonous animals taste **bitter**, and **rotten** food tastes **sour**. So being able to taste sourness and bitterness helps us to avoid toxic or rotten food.

Moreover, our bodies need **sugar**, **salt** and **protein** to survive – if sugar or salt levels in our blood drop too low, our brains can shut down and we die. If protein levels get too low, our bodies stop growing and muscles begin to waste away. So being able to taste **sweet**, **salty** and **savoury** (meaty) things helps us find sugary, salty and protein-rich foods we need. Pretty nifty, eh?

3. (d) in your ears

The main balance organs in your body are found deep within your inner ears. They're called the **vestibular organs**. They lie behind your eardrum and hearing organs, in a chamber next to the brain called the *vestibulum* (Latin for 'chamber' or 'lobby'). Inside are the balance organs themselves – the **otoliths** and the **semicircular canals**.

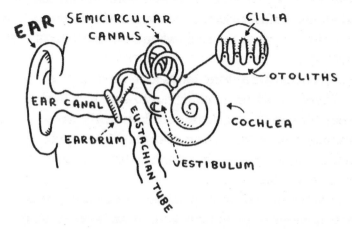

The **otoliths** are little sacs (two in each ear) lined with tiny hairs (called *cilia*), and filled with a gooey, gel-like liquid. Floating in this liquid are a number of tiny solid crystals. Whenever you move your body (and with it your head), the crystals inside the otoliths shift and press against the hairs inside. These send signals to the brain, telling you which way the crystals shifted, and the brain figures out that your head must be moving in the opposite direction. From this, even with your eyes closed, you can figure out if you're **travelling**

forward, backwards upward, downward (including falling) or sideways.

But the otoliths only pick up linear **movement** (or movement in a straight line). To detect **circular movement** (twisting, rolling and rotation of the head and body), you need the semicircular canals. These three semicircular loops sit behind the otoliths. Like the otoliths, they are filled with fluid and tiny movement-sensing hairs. As your head twists and rotates, the fluid inside sloshes about, wafting the hairs about, and sending signals to the brain about the direction of the sloshing.

Since there are **three loops** (one vertical, one horizontal, and one sticking out to one side), between them, the canals can sense rotations in all **three dimensions**. So by putting information from the eyes, otoliths and semicircular canals together, the brain can figure out exactly what your body is up to, and help you maintain your **balance** relative to the ground. People with *damaged* vestibular organs might have trouble keeping their balance, and can feel like they're toppling over even when they're standing still.

4. (b) optic nerve
The optic nerve is actually a huge bundle of nerves that carries information from each individual cell in the retina to the vision centres of the brain. Light shines in through the pupil and falls on the **retina** – a curved sheet of cells at the back of the eye. The cells

within pick out the brightness and colour of the light striking them, and translate them into signals, sent through nerves. These nerves bundle together within the eye, and the whole bundle (known as the **optic nerve**) passes through the retina to the brain. There, the brain uses this information to form an **image** of the world around us, as viewed by the eyes.

In a similar way, individual nerves inside the inner ear bundle together to form the **auditory nerve**, which carries sound signals from the ears to the brain.

5. (c) cochlea
The **pupil** is the dark hole in the centre of your eye, through which all light shines in. Like the opening (or **aperture**) of a camera, the **size** of this opening can be adjusted to let in more or less light. This is why your pupils shrink to tiny dots in bright sunlight, but widen into big black discs in dim light or darkness.

In a camera, spiralling mechanical shutters open and close the hole. In the human eye, this is done by tiny muscles, which surround the pupil like the spokes of a bicycle wheel. These form the **iris** – the coloured region of the eye that surrounds the pupil. The iris is coloured because it contains varying amounts of a protein called **melanin**. Depending on how much melanin your **irises** contain, they might be blue, green, hazel, dark brown, or anywhere in between.

Once through the pupil, light travels through the **lens** behind and is focused on to a sheet of light-sensing cells at the back of the eye. Which, as we've already learned, is called the **retina**.

So the odd one out, here, is the cochlea – which isn't part of the eye at all. The **cochlea** is a tiny, spiralling tube which lies behind the eardrum – coiled into a shape that looks a lot like a snail shell. As sound waves strike the eardrum, they vibrate a set of three tiny bones attached to the back of it (commonly known as the hammer, anvil and stirrup).

These bones pass the vibration to the fluid-filled cochlea, rippling through its spiralling coils. As the fluid inside vibrates, it bends tiny hairs that line the cochlea, which send nerve signals to the brain. The brain assembles these signals and interprets them as **sounds**.

Boom! – that's hearing in a nutshell. Or a snail shell. Whatever.

6. (d) Because our retinas have holes in them
As we've already learned, nerves from each cell in the retina of the eye are bundled together inside the eye, and pass out through the retina as a single optic nerve. Unfortunately, this also *blocks off* a small patch of the retina. Since there are no light-sensing cells on or in the optic nerve, any light striking this little patch is not picked up. This leaves every retina, and every eye, with a 'blind spot'.

So if this is the case, then why don't we see two little dark spots in the world before our eyes? We **should**, but we don't. That's because the blind spot in your left eye and right eye appear in different places in your field of vision. Hence, with both eyes open, each eye sees what the other doesn't. In fact, even with only **one eye open**, your brain **still** finds ways of filling in the blind spot. In short, it looks at the colour and brightness of the patches that surround each blind spot and fills in the details by assuming that what's inside each blind spot looks more or less the same. So if you're looking at a big, green wall – your brain fills in the blind spots with more of the same (i.e. more plain green).

> You can try this for yourself and actually trick your brain by drawing a small spot on a wall (or if you don't want to get into trouble, on a piece of coloured cardboard), then closing your left eye and looking a few inches to the left of the dot with your open, right eye. Do this right, and the spot will seem to disappear, and your brain 'fills in' the blind spot with plain green.

7. (b) far- (or long-)sighted

Older people generally become more far-sighted (or long-sighted) as they age, meaning that they have **trouble seeing things up close**. This is why so many grandparents wear reading glasses. It's not that the letters are too small to see. It's just that even at arm's length, the page containing the letters is too close for their eyes to focus on.

This happens because the lens of the eye gradually

and naturally changes shape with age. Doctors call this *presbyopia* (from the Greek phrase meaning 'old eye'). There's not much you can do to change the shape of the eye itself. But you can wear corrective glass or plastic lenses (i.e. glasses or contact lenses) in *front* of the eye to focus the light

101 WAYS T OIL YOUR BITS

beams entering the eye in a different way. More recently, some older people have been opting for **laser surgery**, which uses laser beams to reshape the **cornea** (a curved, transparent lens which lies in front of the pupil). This aims to restore normal sight without the need for glasses or contact lenses.

Near (or **short**-)**sightedness** is not usually related to ageing, but is caused by other factors, like damage to the eye muscles, or being born with a slightly misshapen eye lens.

And although it can be caused by strokes and brain damage, **colourblindness** doesn't happen with age either. It is usually genetic – you're either *born* with it, or you're not.

Night-blindness – the inability to see well in dim or low-light conditions – isn't usually age-related either. It's often the result of not getting enough zinc in your diet, which affects the function of rod cells in the eye.

8. (d) Fifteen or more

We often talk about 'the five senses' – sight, hearing, smell, taste and touch. But in reality, humans have at least fifteen more senses, bringing the total to twenty or more. These include sensitivity to **pain**, **temperature**, **pressure**, **itching**, **balance**, **hunger**, **thirst**, **muscle position** and even **electric** and **magnetic** fields.

Pain sensors (or *nociceptors*) are found throughout your skin, and in the tissues that surround your joints and organs. Hot and cold-sensing *thermoceptors* are spread throughout your skin too. (That said, you have more in your hands and feet than you do in your knees and elbows. Which is why your fingers and toes feel hottest when you slip into a scalding-hot bath.)

Baroreceptors in the walls of your blood vessels send signals to the brain when your veins and arteries swell and stretch, allowing your body to get a rough measure of the **blood pressure** within. In turn, this contributes to your sense of **thirst**, as your brain reacts to low blood pressure with a request for more water. Stretch receptors in your stomach trigger your sense of **hunger** and **satiety** (fullness), while still more stretch receptors in your muscles and tendons help your brain to tell how your body and limbs are positioned – an extra sense called **proprioception**. And as we've already seen, your *vestibular organs* help maintain your sense of **balance**.

Incredibly, it seems that human beings also have **electroreceptors** and **magnetoreceptors**, which allow us to sense electromagnetic fields. Although we're not as good at it as whales or pigeons – and we're still not quite sure where these receptors are – tests have revealed that, with training, most people can use these to tell which way is (magnetic) north without a compass!

9. (b) deafness

The auditory nerve is the major nerve bundle that runs from the inner ear to the brain. **Damage to the auditory nerve – which can happen during a stroke or a head injury – can lead to deafness or hearing loss**. In this case, there's nothing wrong with the ears themselves. They're still able to pick up soundwaves and transmit them to the eardrum and cochlea, and turn them into nerve signals. But without a working auditory nerve, these signals can't get to the brain, so the brain can't 'hear' them.

Other important sensory nerves are the **olfactory nerves** (which relay signals from the nose to the brain), the **optic nerves** (which send signals from the eyes to the brain) and **gustatory nerves** (tongue to brain). Again, strokes and head injuries can damage any of these, temporarily (or even permanently) removing your sense of **smell**, **sight** or **taste**.

More good reasons to (a) eat healthy food, (b) avoid smoking, and (c) wear a crash helmet when you ride a bike . . .

10. (b) rods and cones

The two major types of light-sensing cell in the retina of the eye are called rod cells (or simply rods) and cone cells (or cones). Rod cells contain the light-sensing protein **rhodopsin**. When a beam of light strikes a rhodopsin protein, it changes shape and triggers a nerve signal to the brain. If the light is bright, then more signals are sent per second. If it's dim, fewer signals are sent. All sighted animals have rod cells, allowing them to tell the difference between light and dark, and see in shades of grey.

Cone cells, as we've already seen, come in three types, and allow us to make out light of different wavelengths or colours.

Most animals only have one or two types of cone cell, meaning that they can't see as many colours as humans. Some insects and reptiles, though, have a **fourth** type of cone cell which detects **infrared light** that is invisible to humans, allowing them to track prey in the dark. And some birds have a fifth type of cone cell, which can pick out **ultraviolet light** – also invisible to humans. So they see the world in shades we cannot see!

B PICTURE PUZZLE 1

The correct order is:

C (domestic cat)

B (walrus)

D (human)

A (sperm whale)

At just 5cm across, and weighing **30g**, the **cat** has the smallest brain of them all. The brains of pet cats are about 25% smaller than those of wild cats. (The one in the picture is Austin – one of my own two pet cats. Judging by his general level of dippyness, his brain is probably smaller still.)

Next comes the **walrus**, with a brain weight of about **1.1kg** (2.4 pounds). It has the largest brain of any carnivore (including lions, tigers and other predators).

A little larger is the brain of a **human**. On average, an adult human brains weigh about **1.3kg** (3 pounds) – about the same as a bunch of *bananas*. Which makes sense, given that some people are, quite clearly, bananas.

The largest of the bunch is the **sperm whale**. It has a brain that weighs up to **9kg** (or 20 pounds), making it the largest known brain of *any* animal species, living or dead. (The brain of the much larger **blue whale** weighs less, at 'only' **5kg**, or 13 pounds.)

It's worth noting that the biggest-brained animals aren't necessarily the smartest. After all, few people would argue that sperm whales are smarter than humans. Huge animals grow huge brains partly because they have a huge everything. Then again, who knows how smart a sperm whale really is . . .

C: QUICK-FIRE ANSWERS

11. **Ear**. The *tympanic membrane* (or *tympanum*) is the medical name for your *ear drum*.
12. **Nose**. *Olfactory cells* line the inside of your nose, and contain the *olfactory receptors* you use for *olfaction* (smelling).
13. **Eye**. The cornea is a thin, transparent layer that covers the *pupil* of your eye, and helps direct light on to the *lens* behind it.
14. **Mouth**. Your salivary glands make saliva, which

helps you to taste and digest food.

15. **Mouth**. It's that strange, dangly thing that hangs down the back of your throat. It helps trigger the gag reflex which makes you cough and throw up when something wedges in your throat. But it also has taste receptors on its surface.

16. (Roughly) **10,000** different smells.

17. **Millions**. The average human nose contains between 5 and 12 million *olfactory* (or smell) *receptors*. Professional 'sniffers' – like cheesemakers and wine-tasters – tend to have more than the average person. They also have more varied *types* of receptors, allowing them to detect more subtle smell differences than the rest of us.

18. **100 times more sensitive.** While it's true that *some* dog breeds might have noses that are 1,000, 10,000, or even 100,000 times more sensitive than ours, on average, most breeds smell 'only' around 100 times better than we do.

19. (Around) **10,000 taste buds**. Children have more than adults (which might explain why adults happily eat sprouts), and professional chefs and wine-tasters might have a few thousand more than most. But no one has *millions* of taste buds. This is one reason why taste is a weaker sense than smell.

20. **10 times**. (See above.)

21. **80%**. Yep – your brain is almost *all* water. Which is why you need to drink so much of it.

22. **20%**. This is when you're sitting about doing nothing. When you're exercising, your muscles

grab more oxygen, so your brain might get less than 20%. When doing a maths exam, your brain might grab more than 20%.

23. **20%**. Your brain is a *hungry* thing. It needs blood for oxygen and energy supply. At rest, it grabs more blood than any other organ. Although again, this can change with exercise and activity.

24. **3 seconds**. In our altered state of consciousness during sleep, time seems to slow down; seconds can seem like hours, and minutes like days.

25. **10%**. Although we typically use less than 10% of our brains *at a given time*, it's a myth that we don't use the other 90% *at all*. We use pretty much all parts of our brains at some time or another. Just not all parts at the same time.

26. **1,300g (or 3 pounds)**. Men's brains are usually slightly heavier, with an average weight of 1,375g, compared with 1,275g for that of the average adult woman.

27. **600 miles**. If all the coiled branches of your nervous system were unravelled and laid out end to end, it would stretch most of the way from London to Inverness!

28. **100 billion brain cells** (or neurons). Roughly the same number as there are stars in our galaxy.

29. **200 mph**. Not all human nerve signals travel this fast. But some do.

30. **200**. People often go on about a dog's sense of smell, forgetting that cats have a great sense of smell too . . .

D: PICTURE PUZZLE 2

D – **Octopus**. It's the only one of the four that lacks the sense of echolocation.

Bats hunt by screaming in ultrasound and listening for the echoes as they bounce off prey like moths. **Dolphins** echolocate by making ultrasonic clicking noises and listening for soundwaves echoing through the water. And although we humans aren't quite as good at it (and can't make ultrasonic noises), we **can** echolocate by listening for bouncing soundwaves.

In fact, with practice, some blind people become so good at echolocating that they can ride specially adapted bikes (with wheels that make clicking sounds) through dense forests – listening for the echoes from trees in order to avoid them!

Octopuses, however, *cannot* echolocate. They have **no ears**, which makes it kind of tricky. On the flip side, they can change shape, change colour and squeeze through holes little larger than one of their eyes. Which isn't bad, I suppose.

E: MORE MEGA-BRAIN ANSWERS

31. (b) the right half

Generally speaking, the muscles in the right half of your body are controlled by the left side of your brain, and vice versa. A band of the brain's outer **cortex** layer (which stretches across the top of the brain like a hair band) sends signals to the muscles of your head, torso and limbs. This region is called the **motor cortex**.

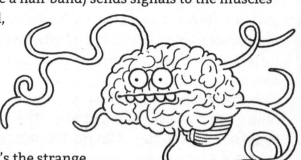

Now here's the strange thing. The brain itself is divided into two halves or **hemispheres**. So half the motor cortex lies on the left side of the brain, and the other half on the right side. You might assume that nerves from each side run straight down through the spinal cord and into the body, with the left motor cortex controlling the left side, and the right motor cortex the right. Right?

Wrong. In fact, we've evolved brains that are wired the wrong way round. Nerves from the **left** motor cortex stretch across to contact muscles on the **right**, and vice versa. So every time your right little finger wiggles, it does so after receiving a signal from the left side of your brain. Weird, eh?

32. (c) motor neuron

There are three basic types of nerve cell (or neuron) in your body.

1. **Sensory neurons** receive information from your skin, muscles and organs, and relay signals to the brain to keep it informed. Touch, taste, smell, hearing, vision, balance and all of our other senses depend upon sensory neurons. They tell the brain what's going on in the world around us. Sensory neurons also tell the brain what's going on *inside* the body, helping it to maintain our blood pressure, organ function and more.

2. The second type of nerve is the **motor neuron**. Motor neurons send information in the opposite direction – from the brain *to* the muscles and organs. While sensory neurons allow the brain to *sense* our bodies and environment, motor neurons allow the brain to *control* our bodies and surroundings. In short, they're how the brain *gets things done*. When our motor neurons stop working (as in sufferers of **strokes** and **motor neuron disease**), we can lose control of our muscles and organ functions.

3. The third type of neuron is an **interneuron**. These form networks and connections within the brain and spinal cord, and are essentially what our brains and **central nervous systems** are made of.

33. (d) a lifetime

Incredible as it might seem, it would be quite possible to survive for an *entire lifetime* with only half a brain. This is because the brain is already cut in half. And if part of one side is damaged, the same region on the opposite side can take over. It's almost like having brain 'backups'.

As we've already learned, the brain is divided into **two separate halves** or **hemispheres**. But what we haven't seen is just how separate they are. In fact, the two halves are barely connected. Take a brain out of a body, and you can jam your fingers in between the two hemispheres with ease.

I'll take your word for it!

Ordinarily the two halves are connected by a bundle of nerves called the **corpus callosum**. This keeps the two hemispheres coordinated and working together. Sometimes, however, the two halves *don't* work well together. Some forms of epilepsy, for example, are the result of both sides of the brain firing at once. To treat this, the corpus callosum is sometimes **cut**, severing the two halves of the brain completely. And guess what? Nothing bad happens. The epilepsy disappears, but the patient is otherwise fine. Left to do its own thing, each half of the brain can stand (and work) alone.

Cases like this have shown us that it's quite possible to survive with just one half of the brain, or the other, intact. In reality, **removing** an entire half of the brain would probably result in severe mental problems, and perhaps some movement problems too. But the point is, you could *survive*, in theory, for as long as anybody else.

34. (c) we have bigger forebrains

Whales and elephants have bigger heads and brains than humans, but that doesn't make them smarter mammals. Humans, however, have weightier forebrains than any other mammal. Specifically, we have billions more cells in the frontal lobes of our brain – the area of the cerebral cortex devoted to reasoning, reflection and complex emotions.

We can't say for certain why this region grew so large in humans, compared with other mammals. Some scientists believe it happened as we started hunting in groups. Others say it grew along with our language ability. Both of these abilities take a lot of reasoning, reflection, emotional understanding and control. So evolving big frontal lobes might have helped us get good at them (and survive better than those with smaller frontal lobes). However we ended up with them, there seems to be little doubt that it's these swollen frontal lobes that makes us so smart. *Most* of us, anyway . . .

35. (d) both (b) and (c)
Between the skull and the brain lie several fatty membranes called meninges, and a layer of watery goo called cerebrospinal fluid. Both serve to cushion and protect the delicate **cortex** from impacts and infection. Occasionally the meninges themselves can become infected by viruses or bacteria, causing viral or bacterial **meningitis**. This can be a dangerous disease, as it causes the membranes to swell and press against the brain, with harmful (or even lethal) effects.

Strong impacts, too, can be dangerous for the brain. Falls, car crashes and heavy blows to the head can cause **concussions** – rattling the brain against the inside of the skull, and damaging brain cells. Worse yet, this can sometimes turn into **compression**. When this happens, the bruised meninges swell up, cerebrospinal fluid builds up beneath the skull and the brain itself is squeezed down towards the neck, causing permanent brain damage or death.

This is why it's so important to wear protective headgear when riding bikes and skateboards, and when playing contact sports. Wearing a bulky helmet might not feel so comfortable. But it's definitely more comfortable than having your brain squeeze itself down your neck . . .

36. (b) the wrinkles shorten the connections between different parts of the brain

The outer part of the human brain – known as the **cerebral cortex** – is covered in folds or wrinkles called *sulci*. If you removed the cortex layer and unfolded it, it would make a single sheet with an area of roughly **2,500cm² (2.5 square feet). WOW!** Interestingly, these wrinkles are missing in **primitive mammals** like mice and shrews. The brains of cats and dogs are a little more wrinkly. But only higher primates (chimps, gorillas, bonobos and humans) have *really* wrinkly brains.

This tells us that the wrinkles are there for a reason. Somehow, the wrinkles seem to make us smarter than other animals. But how?

Neuroscientists think they've figured it out. The wrinkles and folds, they say, scrunch different parts of the cortex together, allowing connections which otherwise could not exist to form between different parts of the brain.

So there you have it. When it comes to brains, the wrinklier the better.

37. (d) all of the above

We still don't fully understand **how** sleep works. But by keeping people awake for days on end and observing the effects on their brains and behaviour, scientists have at least figured out some of the reasons why we need sleep, and what happens when we don't get it.

During sleep, the brain goes into a kind of 'standby' mode. Since the body is hardly moving, there is hardly any activity in the movement (or motor) centres of the brain. And since we're not actively thinking or working things out, the reasoning and learning centres also become far less active. This allows the brain to process information it has stored from the previous day — attaching new memories to old ones, making comparisons between them and filing it all away for future use.

We know this because when scientists keep people awake in so-called **sleep-deprivation experiments**, they don't do so well on memory tests. They also **learn** things (including lists of facts and figures and new physical skills like juggling) far **more slowly**. This is hardly surprising, since learning depends on memory formation. If you can't remember how to do something, how are you supposed to get any better at it over time?

Brain scans of non-sleeping people also reveal that the brain repairs itself while we sleep. It grows new neurons, repairs leaky blood vessels and grows new connections (synapses) between the billions of neurons it already has. This happens during our waking

ZZZ

TEST PAPER

hours too. But it happens far more rapidly during sleep. It's a bit like powering down your computer so that you can insert new memory chips, repair frazzled circuits and install new software. Without sleep, your brain becomes muddled, outdated and far less powerful. So make sure you get yours!

38. (a) altered blood flow to the brain

'Brain freeze' (or 'ice-cream headache') happens when you eat frozen food or drink a frosty milkshake, which draws the heat from the roof of your mouth (or **palate**). Just above the palate lie a series of blood vessels leading to and from the eyes and brain. When these blood vessels get cold, your body assumes that the rest of your body is just as cold – as if you've suddenly fallen into an Arctic ice-hole. It panics, and the vessels respond by dilating (or widening) to try to increase blood flow to the brain. As the vessels widen, stretch receptors in the vessel walls trigger pain signals to the brain, making your head and eyeballs ache.

Moments later, the ice cream melts, and warmth flows back in the blood vessels. The body realizes it was all just a false alarm, the blood vessels shrink back to their normal size and the pain disappears.

If you want to make an ice-cream headache disappear faster, sip some warm water, or just press your tongue to the roof of your mouth.

39. (b) 5–10 minutes

The brain is a *hungry* thing, using up more of your available oxygen than any other organ. Deprived of oxygen, it can't survive for long. **After just 4–5 minutes without oxygen, the brain begins to die.** Brain cells (or neurons) die off in their millions, and whole areas of the brain shut down. **After 10 minutes without oxygen, the brain is usually damaged beyond repair,** and **death** is the result.

How is it, then, that some people – including sponge divers, free divers and magicians – can hold their breath for 10 minutes or more, and survive unharmed? Peter Colat, a Swiss-born free diver, once held his breath for **19 minutes and 21 seconds**. So what's going on here?

Firstly, holding your breath doesn't cut off the brain's oxygen supply immediately. On a full breath, the lungs contain up to **5 litres** of air. So for a good while after the diver stops breathing, the brain is still using that. *How long* the diver can survive on that breath then depends on *how relaxed* they are, and *how*

123

efficiently his or her body uses oxygen.

If your muscles are tense and your limbs are pumping away, you burn through your available oxygen very quickly. No one could hope to hold their breath for more than a couple of minutes in this state. But if the muscles are relaxed and the breath-holder stays still, *far* less oxygen is used up by the muscles, leaving more available for the brain. With training, divers and magicians can learn to relax their muscles very deeply, doubling, tripling or quadrupling their total breath-hold time.

Training also alters your **metabolism** (how efficiently your body's cells use oxygen). Some people (including most champion divers) are born with lower metabolic rates than others – meaning that their bodies create, store and use energy more efficiently – so they need less oxygen to keep their bodies 'ticking over'. Certain types of training can lower your metabolism even further, resulting in epic, record-breaking, 10–20-minute breath holds.

40. (d) up to 100,000
Tests on thousands of patients have revealed that most people have between 50,000 and 100,000 thoughts per day. The average number of daily thoughts – as far as we can tell – is around **70,000**. Most of these come and go in less than a second, so we might not *remember* more than 10% of our individual thoughts. But clearly, there's a whole lot of thinking goin' on . . .

SENSORY PUZZLER SOLUTION

ANSWERS

PART THREE: EARTHQUAKES, VOLCANOES AND NATURAL DISASTERS ⚡

SUPERGEEK: ANSWERS

>>>>>>>>>>>>>>>>>>>>>>>>>>>>>>>

A: MEGA-BRAIN ANSWERS

1. (d) the United States of America
The largest volcano in the world lies beneath Yellowstone National Park, Wyoming – right in the centre (well, a little way northwest of centre) of the United States of America. The **Yellowstone Caldera** (aka the **Yellowstone Supervolcano**) is a wide, shallow dome that sits atop a vast pool of underground magma that measures over 300 miles (480km) across. According to geologists, the supervolcano has exploded at least three times in the last 2 million years – the last time around 600,000 years ago. And it seems overdue for another MEGA-ERUPTION SOON.

When it does finally blow, it will do so with the force of **1,000 nuclear bombs** (of the kind dropped on Hiroshima during World War Two) **every second**. This could lay waste to an area 1,000 miles in every direction, covering most of the western and central states. It would also cause havoc around the globe, as air traffic would be grounded by immense ash clouds spewed into the atmosphere. And it might even affect global climate, plant life and animal life, by shrouding the Earth in dust for a year or more.

Scientists at the US Geological Survey have been watching the volcano carefully since 2004, when the

>>>

caldera (the dome of earth above the volcano) began rising at over 8cm (3 inches) per year – the fastest rate since records began in 1923. For now, they say, there are no *immediate* signs of an eruption. But in theory, it could go up at any time. And woe betide anyone within 1,000 miles of it when it does . . .

2. (b) earthquakes

Seismometers get their name from the Greek words for 'shake' (*seismo*) and 'measure' (*metron*). Geologists use them to measure seismic waves – vibrations through the ground created by earthquakes and volcanic eruptions.

The oldest versions of these were built by ancient Chinese inventors and featured a central weight or pendulum that would drop, roll or swing in response to an earth tremor. Modern seismometers are more like microphones. They use springs attached to electronic sensors to detect the tiniest vibrations in the earth.

Scientists sometimes leave seismometers – along with temperature gauges, tiltmeters and other devices – atop (*or even inside*) volcanic craters, to detect the tell-tale tremors that warn of a coming eruption. Sadly, even with the best early-warning devices we have today, predicting earthquakes and eruptions is still a tricky business. Fewer than 50% of eruptions – and 10% of earthquakes – are predicted more than a few hours in advance.

3. (a) a vulcanologist

Vulcanology is a branch of geology relating to volcanoes and volcanic activity. Scientists who study this are known as vulcanologists. This is one of the more dangerous scientific jobs in the world. To get close enough to study a volcano, vulcanologists often have to work in fire-retardant suits, helmets, gloves and boots. These help protect them from the searing heat around lava flows, which can reach anywhere from 450 to 1,000°C (840–1,800°F). Some also have to wear gas masks, to help them breathe through the suffocating, sulphurous fumes.

> You might wonder why it's 'vulcan-ologist', and not 'volcan-ologist'? Well, the word 'volcano' comes from Vulcan, who was the ancient Roman god of fire and blacksmith to the gods. According to Roman legend, volcanoes were the chimneys of Vulcan's fiery underground forge. So there you go.

4. (c) lava flows above ground, magma flows below ground

Lava and magma are both types of hot, molten rock. Magma flows beneath the surface of the earth, flowing between gaps and cracks in solid rock as it makes its way to the surface. When magma breaches the surface and flows into the open air or ocean, it is known as lava. Volcanoes build up above pools of magma which ooze or erupt through holes in the earth's crust, forming lava flows that solidify into solid domes and cones.

When magma is exposed to air or water, it reacts with it, forming various types of volcanic rock. Magma and lava have a slightly different chemical make-up and can contain different types of crystals and minerals. For the most part, though, the only real difference between magma and lava is which side of the ground they're on.

5. (d) Indonesia

Of these four countries, Indonesia has the most volcanoes – over 170 in total. Whoa! It also has the highest number (around 130) of *active* volcanoes in the world. The volcanoes of Indonesia are part of the so-called '**Ring of Fire**' – a huge ring of volcanic hotspots that lie at the edges of the enormous Pacific Plate. Ouch! The top of this ring stretches from Alaska's Aleutian Islands to Japan and the east coast of Asia. From these, it runs down through the

Philippines, Indonesia and New Zealand before looping back up via the west coast of South America.

More than 75% of the world's active and dormant volcanoes lie within the Ring of Fire. These include **Mount Pinatubo**, **Mount Fuji**, **Mount St Helens** and the legendary **Krakatoa**, which killed over 300,000 people and sent shockwaves around the world when it exploded back in 1883.

6. (a) because earthquakes cause tsunamis
Earthquakes and *tsunamis* (tidal waves) tend to happen together because it is usually an underwater earthquake that causes a tsunami.

As you might know, earthquakes happen when huge slabs of the Earth's crust (called tectonic plates) slip and grind against each other. When the boundary between these plates lies beneath a landmass, the shockwaves released from the juddering plates cause tremors and earthquakes.

But when the boundary lies beneath an ocean, the juddering plates act like huge paddles, transferring the energy of their movement to the millions of tonnes of water above them. This creates a series of massive, heavy waves, which grow larger as they slide up the sea floor and approach land. Most tsunami waves hit land like a sudden high tide, causing widespread flooding and damage to houses and cars. But some – like the ones that struck Indonesia and Sri Lanka in 2004 – grow into monster waves several metres high,

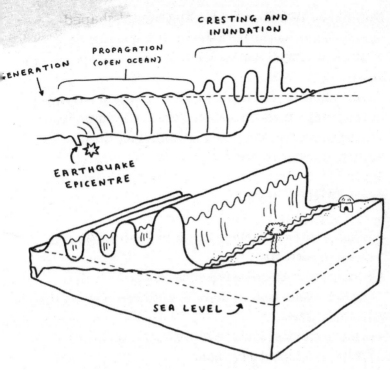

CRESTING AND
INUNDATION

PROPAGATION
(OPEN OCEAN)

GENERATION

EARTHQUAKE
EPICENTRE

SEA LEVEL

sweeping entire houses away and drowning thousands
of people, all at once.

Thankfully, not *all* undersea earthquakes cause
tsunamis. Nor are *all* tsunamis caused by earthquakes.
Some are the result of underwater landslides,
explosions or volcanic eruptions.

7. (d) they're born from different oceans

Hurricanes, **typhoons** and **cyclones** are all
different names for the same thing. Technically

they're all *tropical cyclones* – huge spiral-shaped superstorms that form in the tropics and can cause widespread flooding and destruction as they pass over land.

All tropical cyclones draw their energy from water evaporating off warm waters close to the equator during the summer or early autumn months (a stretch known as a hurricane or typhoon season). But depending on which ocean they form in, they are given different names.

- When a tropical cyclone forms in the Atlantic, it is called a **hurricane**.
- Hurricanes typically strike the coasts of Mexico, the Caribbean islands and the southern coast of the United States.
- When a tropical cyclone forms in the northwest Pacific, it is called a **typhoon**.
- Typhoons typically strike land in Japan, the Philippines and coastal China.
- When they form over the Indian Ocean, they are simply called **cyclones**. Cyclones typically strike land in India, southeast Asia, Madagascar and coastal Africa.

So there you have it!

8. (d) all of the above

Hurricanes bring destruction to coastal communities in **all of these ways**.

The **winds** beneath a hurricane scream around at between **74 and 150 mph (120–240km per hour)**, with sudden gusts that can reach **200 mph (320km per hour)** or more. This is enough to flip cars, rip off roofs and demolish flimsy shacks and houses.

Hurricanes also bring **torrential rains**. Some have dumped over **60cm (2 feet)** of rainfall in a matter of hours. This is enough to flood homes and float cars off driveways.

Coastal towns get hit worst of all by hurricanes, as they also suffer **surging waves** (known as 'storm surges') that can flood entire neighbourhoods and turn roads into rivers. During an especially powerful hurricane, sea levels can rise temporarily by **6m (20 feet)** or more. This is part of what made Hurricane Katrina – which flooded the city of New Orleans, USA, in 2005 – so deadly. In fact, more than half the deaths caused by hurricanes are caused by flooding and storm surges.

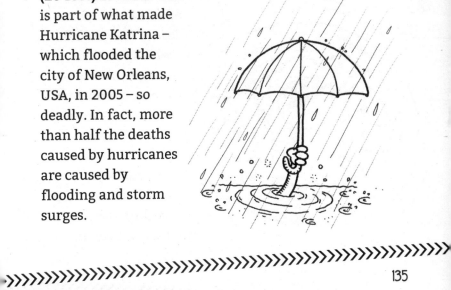

9. (d) all but one of them

Tornadoes happen on six of the world's seven continents. They've been spotted in North America, South America, Europe, Africa, Asia and Australia. In other words, *everywhere but Antarctica*, where the air is just too cold to sustain them. That said, they are *far* more common on some continents than others.

North America gets more than its fair share. In an *average* year, around **1,200** tornadoes strike the United States and Canada. This is partly due to its climate, and partly to its geography. Warm air from the Gulf of Mexico is funnelled across the deserts of the southwest and into the great central plains of North America. There it becomes trapped by the tall Rocky Mountains to one side, and feeds large spinning storm systems throughout the midwestern states.

When conditions on the ground are just right, these storms cause spiralling cylinders of air to form close to the ground, which can then angle upward to become the fast-moving, vertical air columns we know as **tornadoes**.

Of course, these spiralling storm systems *can* form in

Asia, Europe, Africa, or (almost) anywhere else in the world. But they do so far less often.

10. (b) the Fujita scale

The strength and power of a tornado is measured on the Fujita scale – invented by Professor of Meteorology **Tetsuya Fujita** in 1976. The scale isn't really based on how fast the tornado is spinning or moving (as this is pretty difficult to measure without destroying your equipment!). Instead, it's based on the amount of **damage** the tornado does on the ground.

About 74% of all tornadoes are classified as **F0 or F1 – (weak)** tornadoes. These do only light to moderate damage, such as toppling thin trees, caravans and road signs.

Another 25% are **F2 or F3 – (strong)** tornadoes. These cause severe damage – demolishing walls, ripping off roofs, tipping over trains and lifting cars off the ground.

Thankfully, less than 1% of tornadoes are classified **F5 (violent)**. These rare monsters cause **incredible damage**. They strip the bark off trees, rip steel-reinforced buildings from their foundations and toss cars *hundreds of metres* through the air. People and objects swallowed by F5 tornadoes have been found several miles away from where they were picked up.

You do not want to be around when one of these bad boys hits town.

B: PICTURE PUZZLE 1

A – **Arthur's Seat**, which overlooks the city of Edinburgh, Scotland, is an **extinct** volcano. The last time it erupted was over 350 million years ago. So the people of Edinburgh are safe enough!

B – **Mount Etna**, which lies close to the city of Messina, Sicily, is an **active** volcano. According to geologists and historians, it has been erupting continuously for over 3,500 years!

C – **Sakura-jima**, which overlooks the city of Kagoshima, is an **active** volcano. It has been erupting continuously since 1955.

D – **Fuerteventura**, a popular holiday destination in the Canary Islands, is an entire island formed by an ancient volcano. Thankfully, it is **extinct**. Its last eruption happened around 2,500–3,500 BC.

C: QUICK-FIRE ANSWERS

11. There are thousands of volcanoes in the world, but only around **900** of them are classified as 'active', meaning that they have erupted at least once in the last 10,000 years, and show signs that they could erupt again.

    If a volcano hasn't erupted for 10,000 years, but still shows signs of activity (swelling, sudden temperature changes, etc.), it is classified as 'dormant'. Only if it's been more than 10,000 years AND there are no signs of activity is a volcano officially labelled 'extinct'.

12. The South American nation of Chile is home to around **100** volcanoes, of which about 20 are active. These include Mount Chaiten, which erupted in 2008, forcing over 5,000 people to evacuate the nearby town (also called Chaiten).

13. The Philippines, which boasts more volcanoes than any other single country, is home to over **300** of them. Thankfully, less than 10% of these are active. These include the mighty Mount Pinatubo, which created the greatest eruption of the twentieth century when it blew its top in 1991.

14. Believe it or not, Europe is home to at least **60** active volcanoes. Turkey has the highest total number of volcanoes (dormant and active), but Italy is home to two of Europe's most famously

active ones – Mount Etna and Mount Vesuvius.

15. Japan is essentially one big chain of volcanic islands, formed at the boundary of two massive tectonic plates. It is home to around 200 volcanoes, of which a little more than **100** are still active.

16. **2005**. Hurricane Katrina hit the coastal city of New Orleans, Louisiana, on **29 August 2005**, killing 1,422 people and causing 75 billion dollars' worth of damage.

17. **2004**. The 'Boxing Day Tsunami' struck India, Indonesia and Sri Lanka on **26 December 2004**, killing over 224,000 people and leaving 1.8 million more homeless.

18. **2011**. The Tohoku ('Eastern Plains') earthquake struck Japan's east coast on **11 March 2011**. The tsunami that followed did most of the damage, drowning over 13,000 people, and leaving another 340,000 homeless.

19. **2010**. A magnitude 7.1 earthquake hit the impoverished island of Haiti on **12 January 2010**. It killed over 150,000 islanders and left more than 3 million people homeless.

20. **2005**. Two tornadoes ripped through the city of Birmingham on **28 July 2005**. Although no one was killed (and less than 20 people injured), the tornado's 130 mph winds caused over 40 million pounds' worth of damage in a matter of minutes.

21. **USA**. The San Andreas fault runs for over 800 miles (1,300km), along one edge of the state of California.

It marks the boundary of two massive tectonic plates – the Pacific Plate and the North American Plate. Cities built close to the fault – including San Francisco – suffer an unusually high number of earthquakes each year.

22. **Asia**. Tsunami are most common in the Pacific Ocean, which is ringed by a series of tectonic-plate boundaries and volcanoes. Undersea quakes frequently cause tsunami. And although some of these occasionally reach the west coast of the Americas, the vast majority strike Asian coasts and islands.

23. **Africa**. The eastern regions of Africa – from Somalia to Chad, and from Sudan to Kenya – are the most drought-prone regions in the world: so bad that they turn thousands of acres of grassland into desert each year.

24. **USA**. While tornadoes can and do happen on any of the world's continents, North America – and the Midwestern USA specifically – is by far the worst region for severe tornadoes.

Five states (Texas, Oklahoma, Kansas, Nebraska and South Dakota) lie within a 1,500-mile long corridor known as 'Tornado Alley', where thousands of tornadoes have struck over the last few decades. Texas alone has seen more than 8,000 tornadoes since 1950.

25. **Europe**. We English moan a lot about the constant rain and bad weather. But if you look at the big picture, our weather really isn't that bad. Earthquakes, tsunami, hurricanes, tornadoes and other natural disasters are all so rare in northern Europe that they're hardly worth worrying about. Which is more than the *rest* of the world can say . . .

26. **35 mph**. Anything less than that is a mild snowstorm.

27. **74 mph**. This is the minimum wind speed for a Category 1 hurricane. The winds of the most powerful (Category 5) hurricanes can reach double that – over 155 mph.

28. **200 mph**. Avalanches contain thousands of tonnes of heavy snow, so gain momentum quickly as they roar down mountainsides. My advice – don't be in the way when they do.

29. **450 mph**. Pyroclastic clouds are a mixture of superheated gas and rock, which explode from volcanoes during the early stages of an eruption. At 450 mph, there's little hope of outrunning them. Even in a Ferrari.

30. **200 mph**. The winds within an F4 tornado – the second-largest type on the Fujita scale – rage at between 166 and 200 mph. The screaming winds of a monster F5 tornado can reach over 320 mph. Thankfully, F5s are very rare.

D: PICTURE PUZZLE 2

B – **Mount Everest, Nepal** is the odd one out. It's the only one of the four that is *not* a volcano.

Mount Fuji is an active volcano which last erupted in 1707.

Mount St Helens is an active volcano which last erupted in 2008.

Mount Kilimanjaro has not erupted for over 300,000 years, but is nonetheless a dormant volcano.

Mount Everest, on the other hand, is *not* (and never has been) a volcano. It was formed (along with the rest of the Himalayan mountain range) when India collided with the rest of the Asian continent, around 60 million years ago.

E: MEGA-BRAIN ANSWERS

31. (b) Eyjafjallajökull

Eyjafjallajökull (Icelandic for 'mountain island glacier') is a smallish volcano that lies close to the southwestern coast of Iceland, beneath a cap of glacial ice. Although quite active in the early-nineteenth century, Eyjafjallajökull was fairly quiet through the twentieth, leading vulcanologists to believe it might be dormant.

Less than 15 miles (24km) away, in the same mountain range, lies another glacial volcano called Katla, which has erupted at least 20 times in the last 1,000 years (so roughly once every 50 years). Of the two volcanoes, Katla was thought to be the most worrisome.

But all that changed in March 2010, when a series of earthquakes around Eyjafjallajökull showed that it was about to blow. A month later, thousands of tonnes of ash exploded from its main crater, blanketing northern Europe in high-altitude ashclouds. Since jet engines can be damaged when they suck in ash like this, airlines had to ground almost all of their planes for six days while they waited for the clouds to disperse. The eruptions halted in May that year, and since then Eyjafjallajökull has been dormant.

But vulcanologists are still keeping an eye on it, just in case ...

32. (d) people

Put simply, an avalanche is the snowy equivalent of a landslide. Any large amount of snow tumbling down a mountainside can be called an avalanche. Doubtless, they happen all the time in remote mountain regions, with few people around to see it.

Whenever a large layer of snow gets too heavy to support its own weight, there's a danger of it breaking free of the layer beneath, and tumbling downward under the force of gravity, picking up speed as it goes. Sometimes, one layer of snow will slide off the top of an older, more solid layer beneath. This is called a **surface avalanche**. Other times, a whole slab of snow will slide right off the bare rock and grass of the mountainside, all at once. This is called a **full-depth avalanche**.

Sometimes, all that it takes to trigger an avalanche is a *little* fresh snowfall, adding just a little more weight to a huge snow-slab just waiting to slide. Natural avalanches happen more often during snowstorms than on sunny days, for this reason. But over 90% of all reported avalanches (i.e. ones that people see happening) are triggered by people. Between them, skiers, snowboarders, climbers and hikers trigger thousands of avalanches every winter. Often, the person who reported the avalanche is the one who triggered it. Although not everyone survives to tell the tale . . .

33. (d) 10,000,000 tonnes

It's the speed and weight (or the **momentum**) of an avalanche that makes it so dangerous. By the time an avalanche reaches the bottom of a mountain slope, it can contain over 10 million tonnes of snow, rubble and shattered tree limbs – all travelling at up to **200 mph** (320km per hour). YIKES!

Needless to say, you do *not* want to be at the bottom of the slope when this lot arrives. If you're not crushed to death by the impact, you'll be buried so deeply that it'll take hours for rescue workers (assuming they're nearby) to dig you out, by which time you'll suffocate from a lack of oxygen. That's why only 1 in 3 people buried in an avalanche for 60 minutes or more is ever found alive.

34. (a) France

The European Alps are home to the highest number of deadly avalanches each year. This might be because conditions there make snow layers more unstable and avalanches more common. Or it might be because so many more skiers, climbers and tourists visit the Alps each year, compared with other avalanche-prone mountain ranges.

In any case, over **250,000** avalanches happen every year in France, and around a fifth (21%) of all avalanche deaths worldwide happen in the French Alps.

Another 18% of fatalities happen in the Austrian

Alps, and 16% in the Swiss Alps. Mountain ranges in the USA – notably the Rockies – are home to around 17% of all deadly avalanches. Which is not bad at all if you consider its much larger area and population. Canada gets just 9%, and Norway only 2%. Between them, Germany, Italy and other countries make up the rest.

Which just goes to show: if you want to snowboard *safely*, you should go to Norway!

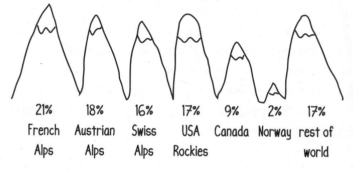

| 21% | 18% | 16% | 17% | 9% | 2% | 17% |
| French Alps | Austrian Alps | Swiss Alps | USA Rockies | Canada | Norway | rest of world |

35. (c) Europe

In total, the great European heatwave of August 2003 claimed over 35,000 lives, including over 14,000 in France, 7,000 in Germany, more than 4,000 in Spain and Italy and over 2,000 people in the UK.

How did this happen? No one knows for sure. But climate scientists say that unusually warm oceans, coupled with stagnant, unmoving pockets of air, sent surface temperatures soaring to over **40°C (104°F)** for weeks on end. In other parts of the world – like Africa, Australia and the southwestern United States – this kind of climate is common during the summer months. But the people of Europe were simply not prepared for it. Elderly people, especially, were unable to recover when air temperatures failed to drop in the evenings. Many succumbed to heat stroke and dehydration long before they could be reached by doctors and ambulances. Of those that died in the disaster, the vast majority were over 60 years of age.

Worse yet, this probably won't be the last time Europe sees this kind of weather. Thanks to the effects of climate change, deadly heatwaves like this could happen every couple of years by the year 2050. Let's hope we're better prepared for it next time.

36. (d) exploding asteroid

On 30 June 1905, an asteroid exploded over Tunguska, Siberia, lighting up the sky like a second sun and destroying over 1,200 square miles of forest in seconds. Happily, there are very few people living in this remote forested region of northwestern Russia. The only witnesses were a few local Tungus tribes, who described the event to researchers years later.

Scientists estimate that the asteroid was just 60m (200 feet) wide, and exploded 5 miles above the Earth's surface after partly burning up in the atmosphere. Had it been a little larger, and arrived five hours later, it would have wiped out the entire city of St Petersburg, killing over 20,000 people. A few hours later still, and it might have hit London – home to around 6.5 million people at that time.

Astronomers reckon there are between 10,000 and 20,000 asteroids measuring 300m or more across (that's five times larger than the Tunguska one) in orbits that take them perilously close to the Earth. One such asteroid – 2009DD45 – buzzed the planet in March 2009, missing us by 'just' 40,000 miles. Few people took much notice.

I hid in the basement, just in case.

37. (c) 10km

From measurements, mathematics and computer simulations, scientists have worked out that the asteroid (or comet) that created the Chicxulub crater was around 10km wide. The impact, which happened around 65 million years ago, at the end of the Cretaceous period, caused an explosion equivalent to over **100 million tonnes** of TNT. Put another way, it released **6 million times** more energy than the explosive eruption of Mount St Helens in 1980. Little wonder, then, that this impact caused global firestorms, sudden climate change and most likely wiped out the dinosaurs . . .

38. (b) 1km

While the Chicxulub asteroid measured 10km across, experts reckon that an asteroid a tenth that size – just 1km wide – would be large enough to threaten all human life on the planet today. YIKES! Impacts from smaller asteroids (100–1,000m across) could wipe out entire cities, or even countries. But 1km is probably the minimum size an asteroid would have to be in order to affect global climate, and wipe out plant and animal species on a *global* scale.

Striking land, a 1km asteroid would trigger massive earthquakes (and possibly eruptions from nearby volcanoes), and throw up a vast cloud of dust, dirt and debris. This dust cloud would then circle the planet for a year or more, blotting out much of the sun's light and warmth, and killing off leafy plants and crops across the globe. In turn, the animals that depend on these for food (including humans) would suffer famine and starvation. Unless you managed to hole up in a well-stocked bunker for at least a year, you'd be pretty much done for.

Even if it missed all major continents and struck the open ocean,

an impact from a 1km asteroid would cause **major earthquakes** and **megatsunami,** and **blast billions of tonnes of seawater more than 1,000km up into the atmosphere.** This would partly destroy the ozone layer, leaving plants and animals vulnerable to deadly UV radiation. In the end, the effect on human life would be more or less the same: **BAD.**

39. (d) both (a) and (c)

Lake Nyos, Lake Monoun and Lake Kivu are all volcanic 'crater lakes', which lie within a few hundred miles of each other in central Africa. (Nyos and Monoun are

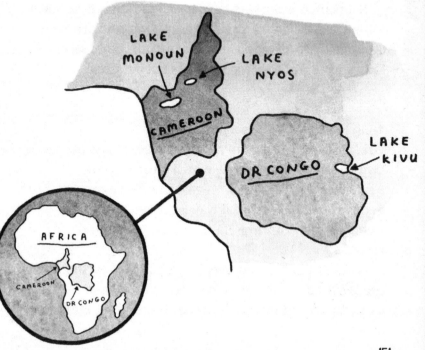

in Cameroon, while Kivu is across the border in the Democratic Republic of the Congo).

These three lakes share a unique and deadly feature. They are all fed by underground pockets of magma which release toxic carbon dioxide into the water from below. This reacts with the lake water to form carbonic acid, making them acidic. But that isn't the worst of it. Over time, the lakes have become so saturated with carbon dioxide that it occasionally erupts from the lake surface, engulfing nearby farms and villages in invisible toxic fumes. This happened at Lake Monoun in 1984, and at Lake Nyos in 1986, killing some 1,700 people, and over 3,000 farm animals.

Ever since, scientists have been studying these lakes to figure out what caused the eruptions, and are even attempting to 'de-gas' the lakes to make them safer. How successful they have been is not yet clear.

40. (c) 500m (1,640 feet)
The largest tidal wave in recorded history was the **Lituya Bay Megatsunami**, which struck Lituya Bay, Alaska, in July 1958. Megatsunami are rare and freakishly large tidal waves caused by massive earthquakes, eruptions, landslides and asteroid impacts.

At Lituya Bay, a massive, magnitude 8.1 earthquake broke over 30 million cubic metres of rock and ice off a nearby mountainside, and sent it tumbling into the bay below. As the enormous mass of rock splashed into the ocean, it created huge ripples that grew into a monster wave over 500m tall. The megatsunami ripped into the bay – swallowing fishing boats and clearing trees more than **900m (3,000 feet)** from the shore, leaving only empty rock behind. Thankfully, almost no one was living in the area, and only five people (mostly fisherman) are known to have died as a result.

This was the largest megsatsunami in recorded history, although we have evidence that other, larger ones happened before human civilizations arrived on the planet. The megatsunami caused by the Chicxulub asteroid impact, around 65 million years ago, was probably over **3,000m** (almost **10,000 feet**) high, and flooded lands from Mexico to Madagascar!

DISASTER PUZZLER SOLUTION

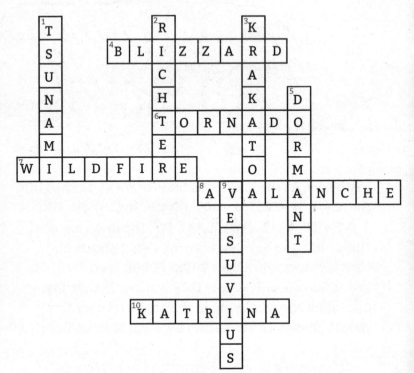

ANSWERS

PART FOUR:
PLANES, TRAINS
AND TRANSPORT

SUPERGEEK: ANSWERS

>>>>>>>>>>>>>>>>>>>>>>>>>>>>>>>
A: MEGA-BRAIN ANSWERS

1. (d) engines

The word *aeroplane* is used to describe any powered, fixed-wing aircraft. So gliders – which do have fixed wings, but don't have engines – are not technically aeroplanes. Nor are **helicopters**, which *do* have engines, but *don't* have fixed wings. **Microlights** and **ultralights** *are* aeroplanes. They are essentially fixed-wing hang-gliders with small propeller engines.

Aeroplane engines come in two basic types.

Turboprops are combustion engines similar to those found in cars and other vehicles. They burn fuel to drive pistons, which in turn drive a spinning driveshaft. In a car, this spinning motion is transferred to the wheels. But in a turboprop aeroplane, it's transferred to one or more external propeller blades, which drive the aircraft forward through the air.

Jet engines are a little different. They have internal

>>

fan blades which compress air, mix it with jet fuel,
then ignite the mix, creating an explosion that drives
a small turbine at the back of the engine, and a large,
multi-bladed **turbofan** at the front.

A third type of aeroplane engine is a **rocket engine**.
These are used only on military **rocket planes**, or
space-planes like the recently retired Space Shuttle.
So while microlights and ultralights are the smallest,
slowest types of aeroplane in the sky, Space Shuttles
are without doubt the fastest!

2. (b) lift

There are four basic forces acting on any aircraft:
gravity, **lift**, **thrust** and **drag**.

Gravity pulls the aircraft down towards the Earth,
just as it does everything else with mass.

Thrust is produced by the aeroplane's engines –
be they propellers, jet engines or rockets. This is the
driving force that pushes an aircraft forward through

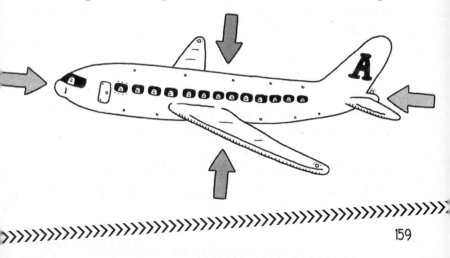

the air, directing high-pressure air past the wings.

Drag is produced by friction between the air and the aircraft's body. Drag pulls back on an aeroplane, opposing thrust and slowing it down. If an aircraft cannot produce enough thrust to overcome its drag, it won't be able to move forward, much less get into the air.

The final force in this set is **lift**. In an aeroplane, lift is generated by air striking the underside of an angled wing. As the high-pressure air is deflected downward, the wing itself is deflected upward. Provided that the aircraft (and therefore the air rushing past the wings) is moving fast enough, this generates enough upward force (or **lift**) to overcome the downward pull of gravity.

So while thrust provides the force that makes lift possible, it's lift that keeps an aeroplane in the air. Thrust alone couldn't do it. If you don't believe me, try lopping the wings off your aeroplane, then try to take off. You can have all the thrust you want. But without wings, there's no lift. So your chances of leaving the ground are zero.

---

3. (a) because their engines don't work in space
Aeroplanes, as we've already learned, move forward and upward by driving air through propellers (or fans) and against their wings. And that, in a nutshell, is the problem with trying to fly an aeroplane in space. **There's no air.** With no air to push past the propellers of a turboprop, and no air to

compress inside a jet engine, prop planes and jet planes simply couldn't generate thrust in the airless near-vacuum of space.

In fact, without specially modified engines, it's pretty difficult to get a standard aeroplane any higher than 50,000 feet (15,000m) or so – far short of the 300,000-foot altitude where space begins. A few military spy planes have managed to reach 80,000 or 90,000 feet. But these have enormous wings and specially modified air-breathing engines, capable of making headway through the thin air. (At 100,000 feet, the air is 100 times less dense that at sea level.)

Even if they could get into space, conventional aeroplanes would be unable to turn or manoeuvre. Usually the pilot does this by angling the movable **control surfaces** on the aircraft – the rudder, elevators and ailerons – deflecting air one way, and the plane the other. But with no air moving across these surfaces, these don't work either. So the pilot would be unable to steer.

For this reason, even the few **rocket planes** that have made it above 100,000 feet haven't been able to do much more than climb and dive, in a huge arc. To move about in space, a spaceplane (like the Space Shuttle) needs extra control rockets – small boosters that release blasts of gas in one direction, pushing the craft the other way.

So it's not just airline pilots being spoilsports, or that they're not allowed. Even if they *wanted to*, they *couldn't* fly their jumbo jets into space. Sorry.

4. (c) pitch, yaw and roll

If you think about it, an **aeroplane** can be turned on three *axes* (or planes) of movement.

The *first* axis is **nose up** (which starts a climb) or **nose down** (which takes the aircraft into a **dive**). Pilots call this first axis 'pitch'. They adjust the aircraft's pitch by moving the elevators (flat horizontal rudders, usually mounted on the tail).

The *second* swings the nose of the aircraft **left** and **right**. Pilots call this lateral, nose-swinging axis 'yaw'. This is controlled mostly by the left and right movement of the aircraft's rudder.

The *third* rolls the wingtips one over the other, tilting or banking the aircraft to the left or right. Pilots call this wing-tilting axis 'roll'. To make the plane roll, pilots use the long, flat ailerons mounted on the trailing surface of each wing – tilting one up and the other down.

By combining these control surfaces, a pilot can move the aircraft in any direction he or she likes. In fact, planes are usually turned by adjusting the ailerons *and* rudder – banking the aircraft and swinging its nose around at the same time.

5. (a) because they're following the curve of the Earth

Airline pilots follow curved flightpaths across the Atlantic because – believe it or not – *that's actually the shortest path they can take*. But how can that be, since (as we all know) the shortest distance between any two points is a straight line? The answer is that the pilots are following the straightest line they can, without flying through the Earth itself.

Think about it – the Earth is a ball. A huge three-dimensional sphere. So a perfectly straight line between, say, New York and London would plunge into the Atlantic Ocean, tunnel through the Earth itself and approach London from under the ground. Being unable to do that, airline pilots do the next best thing. **They follow the curving surface of the Earth and its oceans, but take the shortest route across the surface** between the two points of departure and arrival.

On a flat, two-dimensional map, this path looks curved. But if you sketched it across a 3D globe, you'd see that this arc is actually the shortest, straightest path you can take. These curving lines are called **geodesic arcs**, and they form the basis of every long-distance flightpath.

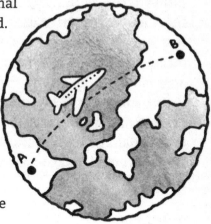

6. (c) it floats above the track

MagLev (short for Magnetic Levitation) trains actually float above their tracks, lifted into the air and propelled along the track by magnets. Powerful, switchable electromagnets line the MagLev track and the bottom of the train itself. A computer controller switches the polarity of the magnets back and forth (a bit like rolling a bar magnet over and over, exposing first its 'north' and then its 'south' end), creating waves of magnetic attraction and repulsion. This lifts the train a few centimetres above the track and drives it forward along the track.

With no contact between the train and track, there is **no friction** with the ground. So the train becomes more like an aircraft, cutting through the air with little (besides air resistance) to slow it down. Because of this, MagLev trains can reach incredibly high speeds – up to **300 mph** or more.

The Japanese JR MagLev managed 361 mph (581km per hour) on a test line in 2007. Experts reckon future MagLevs could double that speed.

7. (b) China

In 2013, the world's fastest passenger train speeds between the cities of Shanghai, Nanjing and Hangzhou, hitting a top speed of **303 mph** (487km per hour).

Speeds of over **450 mph** have been reached by *test*

trains on *test* tracks – without passengers or cargo. So China doesn't hold the overall rail speed record (at least not right now). But it *can* lay claim to the fastest commercial passenger train line.

That said, the Chinese government also recently announced that all trains on this line would be slowed to 186 mph (300km per hour) to reduce the high costs of running the trains.

Booooooo! What kind of fun is that?

8. (c) 460m (1,500 feet)

The longest ship ever built was the *Seawise Giant*, also known as the *Happy Giant*, the *Knock Nevis* and

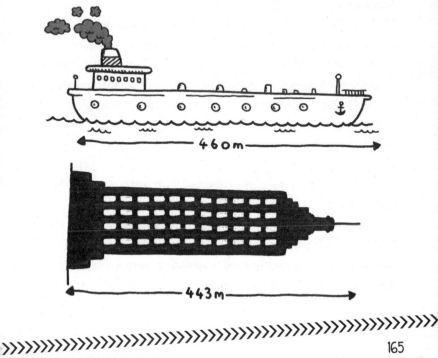

the *Jahre Viking*. It was built in 1976, and changed hands (and names) several times before finally being scrapped in 2010.

This monster oil supertanker measured 460m (1,500 feet) from end to end. That made it longer than the Empire State Building (443m) is tall. It was also one of the heaviest ships ever built, weighing in at over 260,000 tonnes. She had a top speed of 18 mph (30km per hour), but so much momentum that you had to cut off the engines over 5 miles from port to have a hope of stopping her in time.

9. (d) they weigh less than the amount of water they push aside

It seems hard to imagine how something as enormous as a supertanker or aircraft carrier can stay afloat. Fully loaded, such a ship can weigh well over 200,000 tonnes. So why don't they just plummet to the seabed?

Well, it's not because they're built of lightweight materials. To bear the enormous weight and pressure of their cargo, supertankers and aircraft carriers must be built from the strongest steel – not exactly the lightest material around. Nor are they held up with gas-filled balloons. And oil is certainly *not* lighter than air.

It's all down to simple physics, and to buoyancy. In 212 BC, Greek mathematician Archimedes famously discovered the principle of buoyancy, now called the Archimedes Principle in his honour. In short, it goes like this:

As long as an object weighs less than the amount of water it displaces, it will float.

Every object, when immersed in water, pushes some water aside. If you are that object, and you're jumping into a full bath, the displaced water flows over the side and on to the floor. In the ocean, this water is simply pushed aside by the hull of ship. In any case, that volume of displaced water *weighs* something.

DOG IN

WATER OUT

If the ship weighs more than the volume of water its hull pushes aside, it will sink. If it weighs the same, or less, it will float. Even if that particular ship weighs 260,000 tonnes.

That's why oil tankers have such huge, deep hulls (the bottom of the *Seawise Giant* sat more than 80 feet below the waves). They have to push aside a volume of water that weighs more than the ship itself.

In theory, you could float an entire *city* on the ocean, given a wide, deep and strong enough hull. Maybe we'll have to one day, if global warming keeps going the way it is . . .

10. (b) it rises

Submarines dive (submerge) and rise (surface) by adjusting their weight and buoyancy in the water. All subs have hollow chambers called ballast tanks, which lie between the ocean-facing hull and the rooms and chambers for the crew and engines. At the surface, these tanks are filled with air, helping to keep the sub buoyant and afloat. When the captain wants to dive, he signals the crew to fill the ballast tanks with water. This makes the submarine heavier, but its overall volume stays the same. So the sub (temporarily) weighs more than the volume of water it displaces, and it sinks.

When the captain wants to surface, he signals the crew to fill the ballast tank with air (kept in compressed-air vessels for just that purpose). This pushes out the heavier water and makes the sub lighter. Again, the sub's volume has stayed the same. But because it is now lighter than the volume of water it displaces, it becomes more buoyant and floats upward. Simple.

Let's hear it for Archimedes. HIP HIP HOORAY!

Without him, we wouldn't have monster tankers *or* submarines. What a sad loss for the world that would be.

A – **Wright Flyer**. This is the aircraft built and flown by the Wright Brothers, who famously made the world's first heavier-than-air sustained flight.

B – **Spirit of St Louis**. This was the modified *Ryan M-2* turboprop aeroplane which Charles Lindbergh used to make the world's first non-stop solo flight across the Atlantic Ocean – from New York to Paris – in 1927. He became a national hero, and won a cash prize of $25,000 for his efforts.

C – **Spitfire**. The *Supermarine Spitfire* was the most famous fighter plane of World War Two. Tens of thousands were built and flown in high-risk missions over France, Germany and the English Channel. Fast and highly manoeuvrable, Spitfires played a key part in winning the battle against the German Luftwaffe for the skies over England – known to historians as the Battle of Britain.

D – **Blackbird**. The *Lockheed R-71 Blackbird* was a sleek, superfast spy plane built by the American military during the 1960s. In a 1971 test flight, it set the record for the fastest air-breathing (or non-rocket) aircraft, reaching a top speed of Mach 2.88 (2,193 mph). That's nearly *three times* the speed of sound!

C: QUICK-FIRE ANSWERS

11. **400 tonnes**.

12. **650 tonnes**.

13. **850 passengers**. A standard A380, divided into first-class, business-class and economy-class sections, carries 523 passengers. But with economy-class seating only throughout, you can cram over **850** passengers inside.

14. **650 mph** (Mach 0.85).

15. **$375 million**.

16. **1930s**. Although helicopter designs had been made as far back as Leonardo da Vinci (who designed his 'aerial screw' around 1480), the first working helicopter wasn't built until 1936. Mass-produced modern helicopters – of the single-rotor shape we know today – didn't really take off (no pun intended) until the 1950s.

17. **1930s**. The LZ-129 *Hindenberg* was a luxury, rigid-frame airship (or Zeppelin) built to carry passengers and cargo across the Atlantic.

On 6 May 1937, it caught fire while attempting to land at Lakehurst, New Jersey, USA. Within minutes, the entire craft had burst into flames and dropped from the sky, killing all 35 passengers and crew. After that, passenger airships were pretty much abandoned in favour of aeroplanes and helicopters.

18. **1930s**. British engineer **Frank Whittle** invented the first jet engine in **1937**. Sadly, the British military ignored his designs for several years. So it was the German air force, during World War Two, who built and flew the first working jet.

19. **1900s**. After several years spent building gliders and test craft, Orville and Wilbur Wright built and flew their famous *Wright Flyer* in **1903**.

20. **1940s**. Daredevil American test-pilot Chuck Yeager first broke the sound barrier (achieving a speed of Mach 1.06, or 807 mph) on 14 October 1947 – flying his experimental *Bell X-1* rocket plane.

21. **763 mph**. *Thrust SSC* (Super-Sonic Car) broke the land speed record on 15 October 1997, hitting a top speed of **763.05 mph** (or Mach 1.002) – *just* faster than the speed of sound at sea level.

22. **456 mph**. The French-built TGV (Train à Grande Vitesse, or 'high-speed train') train reached **456 mph** in a test run (without carriages or passengers) in 1990. Not even MagLev trains have topped that. (Not *yet*, anyway.)

23. **167 mph**. Japanese *Shinkansen* trains (also known as 'bullet trains') tilt and lean into corners (like speedway motorcycles) as they glide along the track, allowing them to corner at speeds of up to **167 mph**. Most conventional trains would leave the tracks (or 'derail') taking a corner at half that speed. (On straight track, Shinkansens regularly hit 275 mph, making the passing landscape a blur.)

24. **318 mph**. A jet-powered hydroplane boat called the *Spirit of Australia* broke the speed record for water-borne craft in 1977, hitting 289 mph, piloted by Ken Warby. One year later, he trounced his own record on a second attempt, hitting an incredible top speed of **317.6 mph**.

25. **167 mph**. In 1990, Dutch cyclist Fred Rompelberg pedalled his custom racing bike to an amazing 167 mph on the salt flats of Utah. This was on *flat* ground, mind you, not rolling down a hill or something. That said, he was riding behind a motor car, which reduced his aerodynamic drag by redirecting air around him . . .

26. **12 seconds**. Yep. The Wright brothers' famous first flight lasted just **12 seconds**, and covered just 120 feet (36m). They had three more attempts that day, though. On the final try, they stayed aloft for just under a minute, and flew 852 feet (260m). Which was far more respectable.

27. **8 minutes**. Space Shuttles take (or rather *took*, since they have all been retired in favour of non-reusable rockets) around **8 minutes** to get from the launchpad into orbital space around the Earth.

The solid rocket boosters used for launch burn for about 2 minutes before dropping off, then the main engines burn for another 6 minutes before cutting out. Rockets and shuttles accelerate from 0 to 60 mph in just under 5 seconds - much slower than a Ferrari. This might be surprising, until you remember that rockets have to go straight up, fighting gravity all the way.

28. **2 seconds**. Some F1 cars have managed it in as little as 1.6 seconds. But the average F1 car takes between **2** and **2.5** seconds to accelerate from 0 to 60 mph.

29. **2 blades**. The most common types of helicopter – small, single-rotor helicopters with two blades on the main rotor – were first designed and built by the Bell helicopter company, based in Texas, USA. These include the *Bell 47* 'bubble' chopper, the multipurpose *Bell 206 Jetranger*, and the *Bell UH-1 Iroquois* (or *Huey*) military chopper. The same company also built the *Bell X-1* rocket plane that first broke the sound barrier.

30. **6 blades**. *Boeing CH-47 Chinook* helicopters are designed for heavy lifting, and are commonly used as military cargo transports. They have two separate engines – one front, one back – with three blades attached to each rotor, giving a grand total of six blades.

D: PICTURE PUZZLE 2

D – **Hydrofoil**. All the others float above the surface they run on. Hovercraft and ground-effect trains float on a cushion of air. MagLev trains levitate above their track using superconducting magnets. But hydrofoil boats, speedy as they are, have wing-shaped blades that cut through the surface of the ocean. The stilted blade lifts the hull out of the water, reducing drag. But it still makes contact with the surface the vehicle runs over – making the hydrofoil the odd one out.

E: MEGA-BRAIN ANSWERS

31. (a) they're all electric cars

The Leaf, the Ampera and the Tesla Roadster are three of the world's best-selling Electric Vehicles (or **EVs**). Electric cars are actually not that new. The idea goes right back to the 1800s, when engineers in Hungary, Scotland and the USA all designed and built 'electric carriages' powered by batteries and motors. By the early 1900s, steam cars, petrol cars and electric cars could all be seen on city roads in the USA – a country that would later become the undisputed home of the motor car.

For many years, heavy batteries made electric vehicles impractical for anything other than driving at low speeds and for short distances. They made good milk floats, airport buggies and motorized golf carts. But compared to vehicles with petrol and diesel engines, they weren't much good for hauling goods, racing down motorways or driving across countries and continents. So between 1930 and 1990, electric cars fell into decline and all but disappeared from the world's roads.

But in the last few decades, electric cars have come *roaring* back. With new, lightweight batteries that can run for 100 miles or more between charges, and powerful, high-performance electric motors . . .

some EVs can even outrun petrol cars of the same size and weight!

The **Nissan Leaf** can run for 100 miles between charges, and uses 70% less energy than an equivalent petrol-powered car. There are already over 100,000 of them on the roads of Europe and the USA.

NISSAN LEAF

The **Opel Ampera** (known in the USA as the **Chevy Volt**) only manages 50 miles between charges. But it also has a backup petrol engine that kicks in when the electric battery runs out, allowing the battery to recharge itself on the move. Thanks to this, it can cover 310 miles (500km) in one go, when needed.

OPEL AMPERA

The **Tesla Roadster** is a luxury, high-speed EV that can cover 250 miles between charges, go from 0 to 60 in 3.8 seconds, and hit a top speed of 125 mph on open road. If you a have a spare £90,000, you can buy one for yourself . . .

TESLA ROADSTER

32. (c) petrol engine and electric motor

Technically, a hybrid vehicle is anything with two or more different types of power source working together. But 'hybrid' usually means a Hybrid Electric Vehicle (HEV). This is a car, bus or motorcycle with a petrol-powered internal combustion engine and an electric motor.

The basic idea of an HEV is to combine the benefits of petrol engines (driving long distances, fast acceleration, quick refuelling) with those of electric vehicles (higher efficiency, lower emissions, less pollution). In practice, hybrid cars switch automatically between their engines and motors at different speeds, allowing the car to combine and recycle energy. The result is that a hybrid uses less fuel overall, and is cheaper to run than most petrol-only cars of comparable size.

Two of the most common hybrid cars on the road today are the **Toyota Prius** and the **Honda Insight**. You've probably seen these rolling around. Maybe your family, or someone you know, already has one.

With petrol getting more and more expensive – and pollution becoming such a problem in major cities worldwide – more and more people are turning to electric and hybrid-electric vehicles. Many car manufacturers are already working on hybrid vehicles that use cleaner, non-polluting hydrogen fuel (rather than petrol) to power their engines and motors.

Maybe one day, all cars will be petrol-free . . .

33. (b) it increases the car's grip on the road

A **spoiler** is basically an upside-down aerofoil (or wing) attached to the back of a car, which redirects air flow and pushes the car downward, increasing its grip on the road beneath. They're typically found on F1 cars, drag racers and other high-performance vehicles. (The little ones you see on everyday city cars do very little and are more or less there for show.)

So why do racing cars, specifically, *need* spoilers? Well, to win races and make quicker lap times, cars have to scream through bends and corners at very high speeds. Ordinarily, the only thing holding a car on the road during cornering is its own weight. If a car takes a corner too fast – and isn't heavy enough to maintain friction between the tyres and track – then it will either spin off the track or roll over completely. Neither of which is very good for the health of the driver.

The thing is that, like aeroplanes, F1 cars are built out of very lightweight materials and are streamlined so that they cut through the air as efficiently as possible. This makes them very fast. But this also makes them rather prone to skidding and rolling during turns. The solution to this is the spoiler. With a spoiler on the back, the faster a car goes, the more the air rushing over the aerofoil presses down on the car – in effect gluing the tyres to the road during fast turns.

In fact, F1 spoilers work so well that if you turned the track and car *upside down*, the car would still stick to it and scream along it without falling off. Provided it maintained a high enough speed. How cool would *that* be to watch during a Grand Prix?

34. (d) it had no driver
'Stanley' is the nickname for a robotic, driverless vehicle designed by the Stanford University Racing Team. Led by Professor Sebastian Thrun – an expert in computer science and artificial intelligence – the team modified a Volkswagen SUV (Sports Utility Vehicle) so that it could *drive itself* through the 130-mile (200km) off-road racecourse, racing against 22 other driverless cars.

The course featured three tunnels and over 100 sharp turns. *Stanley*'s on-board computer used an advanced GPS navigation system to plot its way through the turns, and controlled the steering wheel and gearstick with robotic motors and pistons. *Stanley* took a little under 7 hours to complete the course (giving it an average speed of just 19 mph). But it did so without so much as a scratch or bump, and won its design team a cash prize of over **2 million dollars! $$$!!!**

Since then, a number of car manufacturers and engineering companies have begun working on autonomous (or driverless) cars for public use. Toyota, Audi, BMW, Mercedes and Internet search-engine company Google are all busy building robotic cars, and the first of them could be on our roads within 5 to 10 years.

35. (b) fly

The Transition, made by American engineering company Terrafugia, is one of the world's first practical flying cars. Others – including the **Moller Skycar**, the **Urban XHawk**, and the **Haynes Aero Skyblazer** – have been built before. But none of them has made it out of safety testing and been fully approved for public drivers (and pilots!). The *Transition* isn't quite there yet either. But it soon could be, and looks set to be the first on the roads and in the skies. COOL!!!

Looking more like an aeroplane with wheels than a car with wings, the *Transition* seats two passengers/pilots, each with their own control stick. It can roll happily along roads with its wings folded up, and transform into 'flight mode' in a little under 30 seconds. In the air, the *Transition* uses a single propeller engine and has a range of about 400 miles.

To own one, you'll need to earn a pilot's licence as well as a driving licence, shell out around £200,000 and have space behind your house for a short runway. But hey – all that's a small price to pay for a *flying car*, right?

Whooosh

36. (a) 1981

The first official Space Shuttle mission was launched on 12 April 1981, when the Space Shuttle *Columbia* left our planet's atmosphere and completed its first orbital test flight before coming back to Earth.

Technically, the first Shuttle launched and flown was the *Enterprise*, launched in 1977. But the *Enterprise* (unlike its fictional *Star Trek* equivalent) *never actually made it into Space*. It was carried into orbit on the back of a modified jumbo jet, and flown in the atmosphere to test its manoeuvrability as an aircraft. Later, it was placed on a launchpad and subjected to impact and vibration tests, to help engineers predict how future Shuttles would fare during launch. But lacking rocket engines or heat-shielding, the *Enterprise* wasn't capable of flying into space, much less getting back again.

Columbia flew a total of **27 missions** between 1981 and 2003. But, sadly, it was destroyed during re-entry – on 3 February 2003 – in the second of two tragic Space Shuttle disasters. *Columbia* exploded and broke into pieces while re-entering the atmosphere over Texas, after its heat shield failed and high temperatures ignited fuel inside its wings. The *Columbia* disaster followed the loss of the Space Shuttle *Challenger*, which exploded soon after launch on 28 January 1986.

With two Shuttles lost, the decision was taken to retire the entire Shuttle fleet by 2011 and use alternative, non-reusable rocket designs for future missions.

37. (b) *Intrepid*

NASA began building and testing Space Shuttles in 1977, and launching them in the early 1980s. In all, six Shuttle Orbiter craft were built. In order, these were:

Enterprise	first flight Feb 1977	final flight Apr 2012
Columbia	first flight Apr 1981	final flight Feb 2003
Challenger	first flight Apr 1983	final flight Jan 1986
Discovery	first flight Aug 1984	final flight Feb 2011
Atlantis	first flight Oct 1985	final flight Jul 2011
Endeavour	first flight May 1992	final flight May 2011

The last Shuttle in Space was *Atlantis*, which returned from its final mission on 21 July 2011.

The USS *Intrepid* was a US Navy aircraft carrier, rather than a Space Shuttle. In fact, it was a floating museum which hosted the Shuttle *Enterprise* for a short time after its retirement from NASA service.

38. (c) 17,500 mph

Space Shuttles in orbit travel at around 17,500 mph (28,000km per hour). Military jet fighters can cruise happily at 1,750 mph (Mach 2.2) – or just over twice the speed of sound. The fastest conventional jet in history – the *SR-17 Blackbird* – could hit around Mach 3.2. But no fighter jet could get *anywhere* near a Space Shuttle's orbital speed, which is equivalent to Mach 23. WHOOOOSH!

This super-high speed is made possible by the lack

of friction (and therefore air resistance and drag) in orbital space. With nothing to slow the Shuttle down, it didn't even need to keep its rocket engines burning to maintain orbital speed. In fact, to come back to Earth, the Shuttle had to spin around and fire its engines into the direction of travel. Only then would it begin to lose speed and drop out of orbit.

WHOOSH!

At 23 times the speed of sound, an astronaut on board a Space Shuttle could circle the planet in about an hour and a half – seeing the sun rise and set every 45 minutes. This, of course, played havoc with the astronauts' sleep cycles. But thankfully, most Shuttle missions lasted no longer than a week.

39. (a) friction

Spacecraft, asteroids and other objects 'burn up' as they re-enter our atmosphere because the atmosphere itself is moving – at very high speed – and this generates a great deal of friction when an object ploughs into it.

This might be hard to picture at first. After all, we

all live in the atmosphere, and we're not burning up, are we? But that's because *we're moving too.* Think about it: the Earth has a circumference of around 25,000 miles. And it makes a complete turn every 24 hours. That means (at the equator, at least) any given point on the Earth's surface is moving at (25,000 ÷ 24 =) 1,041 mph. A thousand miles per hour!

And since we are stuck to the Earth by gravity, we're moving at the *same* speed, *all the time.*

Now here's the thing. The Earth's atmosphere – the collection of breathable gases that embraces our planet – is held to the planet by gravity too. So it, too, is moving at over 1,000 mph. So when a rocket or asteroid tries to enter the atmosphere, it grinds up against a huge ball of spinning gases, moving at over 1,000 mph. As the air grinds past the surface of the re-entering object, friction between the air molecules and object surface heats up both the object and the air in front of it. Soon the air around the object reaches a scorching 1,260°C (2,300°F) – threatening to roast the asteroid or spacecraft before it reaches the ground.

Most asteroids do burn up completely in the atmosphere – with only a few (large) ones making it all the way to Earth, becoming meteorites. Space Shuttles and other spacecraft, on the other hand, have **built-in heat shields** – part of a ship-wide Thermal Protection System (TPS) which shields the ship from high temperatures during re-entry.

40. (d) *SpaceShipOne*

The world's first privately owned spacecraft was called (rather unimaginatively) *SpaceShipOne*. It was built by US-based engineering company Scaled Composites, and when it was launched into suborbital space on 21 June 2004 it won the **$10 million** *Ansari-X Prize* for the first private manned spaceflight.

Carried into the high atmosphere by a specially designed launch craft (called *White Knight*), *SpaceShipOne* made a number of test flights between 2003 and 2004. In the most successful, it fired up its single hybrid rocket engine and blasted itself to a maximum speed of 2,170 mph (Mach 3.09) – reaching an altitude of over 112km (the lower edge of orbital space).In October 2004, *SpaceShipOne* was retired and moved to the National Air and Space Museum in Washington, DC, where it still sits today.

In 2009 *SpaceShipOne* was succeeded by another private rocket plane, as part of Sir Richard Branson's Virgin Galactic company. The company hopes to be making regular suborbital spaceflights before 2020, launched from the Virgin Galactic Spaceport in the Mojave desert in California. Hundreds of tickets (costing over £200,000 each) have already been sold for the first flights.

And they named *SpaceShipOne*'s replacement *SpaceShipTwo*! Original!

SPEEDY PUZZLER SOLUTION

HOW TO PLAY SUPERGEEK!

The Rules

However you play the game, you'll need some sort of **timer** to limit the amount of time a player or team has to respond to each question. And if you want to play this book more than once, you'll also need some **blank paper** and **pens**, so you can jot down the answers without scribbling all over the book. For team play, you might also need to nominate someone (the **SuperGeek Quizmaster**) to ask the questions, to time the answers, to note the responses and to sum up the scores.

CHAPTERS

The book is laid out in **four** chapters – each with a separate theme. Each **question chapter** has a corresponding **answer chapter** in the back half of the book.

Each question chapter features the same layout which goes like this:

- 10 multiple-choice mega-brain questions
- picture quiz 1
- 20 quick-fire questions
- picture quiz 2
- another 10 multiple-choice mega-brain questions
- crossword
- Top 10

The **crossword** and **Top 10**s are there just for fun. There are no scores associated with these for normal gameplay. The rest all feature in the game.

Make sure you leave *plenty* of time to read the long answers, as there are loads of fascinating facts in there and you'll learn tons just from going through them.

(If you *don't* have time, and just want to play a quick-fire game, you can always go back and read the mega-brain answers later).

If you're playing solo, you can expect to get through each chapter (responding to questions, then reading all the answers) in an hour or so. If you're playing in teams, it might take a little longer – especially if your team mates spend a long time arguing over the best answer!

SCORING

Scoring the game works more or less the same however you decide to play.

That is:

1 point for every correct answer in the quick-fire and mega-brain sections
• maximum score: **40 points**

2 points for every correct answer in Picture Puzzle 1
• maximum score: **8 points**

1 point for correctly identifying the odd one out in Picture Puzzle 2, and **1 extra point** if you can explain *why* it's the odd one out
• maximum score: **2 points**

Added together, this gives a maximum score of **50 points** per chapter. And since there are 4 chapters in total, the maximum score for the entire book is (50 x 4 =) **200 points**.

Once you have a total score for a chapter, you can see how you did, using the **SuperGeek Scoring Scale** on page 199.

If you complete the entire book and score more than **180** points, you will have earned the title **SuperGeek**. Log on to www.glennmurphybooks.co.uk/supergeek and submit your name, home town and final *SuperGeek* score, and you could earn a place on the **SuperGeek Leaderboard** – updated regularly to show the Top 50 SuperGeeks worldwide. Just think – you could be the **next reigning WORLD CHAMPION of Geek**. Surely, there is no higher honour. Not even a Nobel Prize. After all, you only have to be good at **one** science subject to land one of those . . .

GAME VERSIONS

Depending on how many players you have, there are four basic versions of the *SuperGeek* game. Or rather, four ways to compete using the *SuperGeek* book.

Solo Play

- For this, you'll need a **stopwatch** or **countdown timer** set for 30 seconds, and (unless you just want to circle the answers on the page) a pen or pencil and paper for jotting down the answers.
- On one side of the page, write the numbers 1–20 and 'PP1' (for Picture Puzzle 1) in columns running down the page. On the back, write the numbers 21–40 and 'PP2'.
- Answer each question – reading the question, then starting the timer right away, so that you only have 30 seconds to choose your answer.
- Stop at the end of the chapter, and review the answers.
- Award yourself a mark out of 50, and consult the **SuperGeek Scoring Scale** to see how you ranked.
- At this point, you can either move on to the next chapter, or leave it for another time – keeping your chapter score safe for future reference.
- Once you have completed all four chapters, add up your chapter scores and calculate your final SuperGeek score. If you scored 180 or more, log on to www.glennmurphybooks.co.uk/supergeek and proclaim your brilliance to the world!

Head-to-Head

- For this version of the game, you'll need someone to play against, head-to-head. You'll each need a paper and pen, labelled on each side with the question numbers for the chapter ahead.

- Go through each question, taking turns to read out the question options, and then setting off the 30-second timer.

- Each player writes down their own answer (keep it secret!), and play proceeds until you have completed all 40 questions (plus the two picture quizzes) and reached the end of the chapter.

- This done, the players swap answers sheets, and one player consults the answers, reading out the correct answers, Each player marks the other's answer (with a 1 for the right answer, 0 for the wrong answer, and a 2 for a correct answer on the picture quiz).

- Add up the scores to get the final chapter score, and see who won the round! You can also consult the **SuperGeek Scoring Scale** to see how you both ranked.

- You can play the next chapter immediately, or save your score and play the next chapter another day. Add your chapter scores to get your final SuperGeek score (out of 200), and submit your score to the SuperGeek Leaderboard (www.glennmurphybooks.co.uk/supergeek) if either (or both!) of you scored 180 or more.

Group/Team Play ⬦

- This version of the game is played when you have more than two players. For example, when you're playing as a family of four or five on a car trip, or you have three or more friends over for a *SuperGeek* party. (Hey – if you're going to play, why not make a party out of it?)
- Players can play **individually** (with each person giving their **own** answers) or in **teams of two or three** players (with each **team** agreeing on **one** answer per question).
- Each individual player or team will need their own answer sheet (piece of paper labelled with the question numbers for each chapter), a pen to jot their answers down and something to lean on, like a clipboard or hardback book.
- The game works best if you can nominate one person to be a Quizmaster. The Quizmaster does not play the game. If *everyone* wants to play, you can take turns being Quizmaster.
- In each round, the Quizmaster reads out the question (and answer options) and sets the timer running. If you're playing in teams, allow up to 60 seconds per question, to give time for the players within each team to decide whose answer is right!
- When the time is up, the Quizmaster moves on to the next question.
- Play continues until the players reach the end of the chapter. The players/teams swap answer sheets,

the Quizmaster reads out the correct answers from the answer chapter section, and each player/team marks each question with a 1 or 0. (Or for the Picture Puzzles only, 2.)

- This done, the players shout out their scores for that section, and the Quizmaster writes them down on his/her own piece of paper.
- Winners celebrate, losers mumble and you all decide if you want to play another chapter or leave the next one for another day.
- As before, if you can keep track of your chapter scores, you can add them to get a final SuperGeek score, and players/teams can submit scores of 180+ to the **SuperGeek Leaderboard** (www.glennmurphybooks.co.uk/supergeek).

Classroom Challenge

- This version of the game is designed for entire classes (or 30–40 players) to play at once.
- At the beginning of the game, the players are split into two or more teams, and each team of 10–20 people chooses a **suitably awesome name** for itself. This is very important. After all, if your team is victorious, and ends up on top of the world SuperGeek Leaderboard, you don't want a rubbish, wimpy name up there, do you?
- Each team needs a piece of paper to list their answers.
- From this point onward, the game proceeds just like the team game described above, with the **teacher** (or

other non-player nominated by the class) playing the role of Quizmaster throughout. The Quizmaster asks the questions and times the responses, giving each team up to 60 seconds to argue and jot down their answer.

- At the end of the chapter, the teams swap answer sheets, and the Quizmaster reads out the correct answers (allow plenty of time for this part). Once the teams are done marking each other's answers (1, 0 or 2), they give the answer sheets to the Quizmaster.

- The Quizmaster adds the scores for each team and declares the winners.

- Once more, if you can keep your chapter scores for each round, you can add them after all four rounds are complete to get your team's final SuperGeek score.

- If your team scored 180 or more, log on to www.glennmurphybooks.co.uk/supergeek and submit your (awesome) team name and final score. If you rank in the Top 50 teams in the world, you will be placed on the SuperGeek Leaderboard and revered by every geek on the Internet. Well, at least until someone beats you and knocks you off the list.

SuperGeek Scoring Scale

Final Score	Chapter Score	Rank
180–200	45–50	**SuperGeek** You have reached the very top of the geek food chain. Mere mortals cower at your magnificence, and geeks around the globe strive to be you, even if only for a minute. Congratulations, for YOU. ARE. A. SUPER. GEEK.
160–179	40–44	**Elite Geek** Lesser geeks grovel at your feet, hoping that scraps of knowledge will drop from your incredible brain. You are second only to the SuperGeek in your command of the Geekiverse.
140–159	35–39	**Advanced Geek** You sit far above the average geek, with a mind for facts and an appetite for learning about the world. You are well on your way to geek greatness.

100–139	25–34	**Standard Geek**

Standard Geek
You have an admirable grasp of all things science-y. Good job. But you'll have to learn a lot more if you're to join the geek elite.

70–99	15–24	**Wannabe Geek**

Wannabe Geek
You want to be a geek, but you lack the required knowledge. Read some more Glenn Murphy books, then come back and try again.

0–69	0–14	**Noob**

Noob
Hmmmm. You have a long way to go before you get to claim the title of 'geek'. Good effort, but must try harder.

For more information about Glenn Murphy books, including updates on new releases and titles, check out www.glennmurphybooks.co.uk, or 'Like' us on Facebook at www.facebook.com/GlennMurphyBooks.